God's Faithfulness Fruit:
WALKING THROUGH THE FIELDS OF GRACE AND MERCY IN BLOOM

Compiled By:
Angela R. Edwards

Foreword By:
Rev. Dr. Marilyn E. Porter

Contributions By (in order of appearance):
Mickayla Savage
Reyna Harris-Goynes
Marlowe R. Scott
Maresa Roach
Joanne B. Lewis
Sonya McKinzie
Quin Levy
Faith Makowa
Allaina Maria
Min. Jimmy Merchant
Katina Rice-Davis
Genae Kulah
Precious Damas
Tosha R. Dearbone
Laurie Benoit

Redemption's Story Publishing, LLC, Harlem, GA (USA)

God's Faithfulness Fruit:
Walking Through the Fields of Grace and Mercy in Bloom

Copyright © 2024
Angela R. Edwards

All Rights Reserved.
No portion of this publication may be reproduced, stored in any electronic system, or transmitted in any form or by any means (electronic, mechanical, photocopy, recording, or otherwise) without express written permission from the publisher.
Brief quotations may be used in literary reviews.

Disclaimer: *The following material contains sensitive content that may be disturbing or triggering for some individuals. It is intended for informational purposes only and should not be considered a substitute for professional advice, diagnosis, or treatment. The authors, publishers, and distributors of this material do not assume any responsibility for the consequences of using or misinterpreting the information presented. By proceeding, you acknowledge that you understand the sensitive nature of the content and accept any potential risks associated with exposure to sensitive material. If you find yourself distressed or in need of support after engaging with this content, please seek immediate assistance from appropriate professional services or support networks.*

Print ISBN 13: 978-1-948853-78-1
Digital ISBN 13: 978-1-948853-79-8
Library of Congress Control Number: 2024948793

Scripture references are used with permission from Zondervan via Biblegateway.com. Public Domain.

For information and bulk ordering, contact:
Redemption's Story Publishing, LLC
Angela Edwards, CEO
P.O. Box 639
Harlem, GA 30814
RedemptionsStoryPublishing2020@gmail.com

DEDICATION

This book is dedicated to those who dare to believe in something greater than themselves.

Faith is not merely a concept to be understood but a force to be lived. Let your beliefs guide your steps, inspire your choices, and transform the world.

Your faith can move mountains, heal hearts, and ignite change. Embrace it. Nurture it. Most importantly, act upon it, for it is through your actions that your faith truly comes alive.

ACKNOWLEDGMENTS

First and foremost, I give all glory and honor to **God the Father**. Without Him and His unending love for us all, who knows where we would be? Thank You, Lord, for the precious gift of Your Faithfulness Fruit.

To my supportive and patient husband, **James Edwards:** Words could never express just how much you are loved and truly appreciated. Even amid your health challenges, you continued to fill in the gap as I worked long hours to bring this project to fruition. Thank you for the many meals prepared and for your love. I love you!

To my mother, **Marlowe R. Scott:** I looked forward to writing about the Faithfulness Fruit because of how you demonstrated faith all throughout my life. When you thought I wasn't paying attention in church and in life, I was… observing the ways in which God showed up and showed out in your life. Thank you for instilling in and sharing with me the GREAT FAITH God has gifted to you. I love you beyond words!

To my BFF (Best Friend Forever) and Foreword-writer, **Rev. Dr. Marilyn E. Porter:** Welp! You did it again! Your one account (of countless others) regarding faithfulness shared in your Foreword is powerful! A half-century of friendship cannot go unmentioned, by the way. I'm grateful for you being ever-present when I need you the most, especially when my faith wavers. I love you, Murl!

To the host of Contributing Authors of *God's Faithfulness Fruit* — **Mickayla Savage, Reyna Harris-Goynes, Mom Marlowe R. Scott, Maresa Roach, Joanne B. Lewis, Sonya McKinzie, Quin Levy, Faith Makowa, Allaina Maria, Min. Jimmy Merchant, Katina Rice-Davis, Genae Kulah, Precious Damas, Tosha R. Dearbone, and Laurie Benoit:** I cannot express my appreciation enough regarding each of your phenomenal stories and the impact they will have in the lives of our readership. You removed the excuses and allowed God to use you all in a mighty way. I pray the seeds sown on the pages of this book land on fertile ground and bless at least one on their faith walk. Thank you, thank you, thank you!

Last but not least, to **every person** who reads this book from cover to cover: I ask that you allow God to speak to your "situations" while you operate in faith, even mustard seed size. Move those mountains, in the mighty name of Jesus! Amen and Amen!

FOREWORD

Faith. Faithful. Faithfulness. Faithfully. Faith-filled. Most often, those words are attributed to the character of God (**THE ONE** in Heaven). Now, before you start to *"Mmmmmm Hmmmmm!"* and shout *"Amen!"*, I want you to insert your name in a sentence with those variations existing in the action of faith. Be truthful. Be transparent. Be the only one who truly knows where your measure of faith resides.

Now, let's get back to how God shows Himself to be faithful. First thing first: HE has so much faith in HIS creation of humankind that HE trusts we will ultimately rest all our human ailments and woes in HIS hands. Could it be that HE has more faith in us than we have in HIM?

I am a woman who functions in faith at the high-risk taker level. The only gambling I have ever done consisted of betting on God to always make a way. Almost always, that includes having the faith that I am fully equipped to handle whatever happens while I am standing on the business of faith. Yes, I have learned to have as much faith in myself—the creation—as I have in the Creator simply because I believe in the mastery of His hands.

A few years ago (let's say around 2018), I had some financial "issues." One day, I wanted to get my hair cut, but my bank account was in disagreement with that desire. I sat at my kitchen table and had a little talk with Jesus, explaining to Him the importance of said haircut. After a solid request, I received a very solid response:

"Yes, you can go get your haircut. I got you."

I immediately grabbed my purse (with no money in it at all) and drove to the shop, where I confidently requested a wash and cut. As I sat there waiting for my turn in the shampoo chair, I peeked a few times to see if any money had shown up in my accounts.

They called my name. No money available.

Next up, the dryer (which I knew would take at least an hour). No money available.

Time for the stylist's chair for the actual cut and style. No money available.

I KNEW I heard the voice of God correctly, yet all I saw were zeroes! At the register, after a few minutes of small talk and banter (which I loathe), the receptionist stated, *"That will be $65.00, dear."* I opened my phone to see which account the money miraculously appeared in.

Account one: ZERO. Account two: NEGATIVE ZERO. Account three: A big NOTHING! And then I heard the word "Invoice" ever so gently in my heart. I had forgotten about PayPal because it had been a while since I had sold services. Well, I popped on over there, and according to the timestamp on the email I had received, there was a $3,000.00 deposit paid to the account from an invoice I had sent nearly six months prior. The money had been deposited during that small talk and banter moment just before I was quoted my price. I quickly transferred the funds to cover my bill into my primary account and left a nice tip for the stylist. Not once did I flinch. Not once did I expect to be left hanging. I was 100% sure my faith in my ability to hear clearly from God had activated the favor attached to faith.

Disclaimer: I do not recommend doing something like that unless you have that kind of "crazy faith."

Most are very familiar with the scripture that begins with *"Now faith…"* (Hebrews 11:1). The translation of the word "now" in the original language is "already." Think about that! "Already faith" is the evidence of things not seen! My God! The power in that is remarkable! It literally says that what you stand in faith for is already done; you just have not seen it yet.

Let the church say, *"Amen."*

Faithfulness as a Fruit of the Spirit is a powerful gift of love and courage that is given to God's creation. Note that I did not say "the people of God." That is because you can be an atheist and have faith in something, and faith will do what it is designed to do – show up in the space in which the thing is already done! You see, faith is not restricted to the believer of Christ. Faith is given to the power of having faith. It is that which God has already sanctioned to be so.

Angela – my friend and confidant – I have seen you walk out the faith walk for many years, including the years when we didn't even really understand faith in God, yet our hearts always had a knowing that our minds now perceive as faith. We didn't always see faith exhibited. In fact, we likely witnessed more fear than faith, yet here you and I stand – reveling in the favor of being faith-filled, faithful, and faith-forward! Keep standing on faith and frolicking in the favor that follows the Fruit of Faithfulness.

Rev. Dr. Marilyn E. Porter
The Pink Pulpit International
Connection of Women in Ministry

INTRODUCTION

There's a tree in the garden of spiritual growth that is precious and rare, and its fruit is called "Faithfulness." As you read the pages of *God's Faithfulness Fruit,* you will embark on a journey through the lives of 17 individuals who have tasted that sweet produce of unwavering faith in God. Their stories, as diverse as the branches of a mighty oak, all stem from the same root: a deep-seated belief in God's enduring presence and promises.

Faith, as described in Hebrews 11: 1, is *"the substance of things hoped for, the evidence of things not seen"* (KJV). It is the seed from which all spiritual fruit grows, and faithfulness is perhaps its most enduring harvest. In Galatians 5:22-23, the Apostle Paul lists faithfulness among the Fruit of the Spirit, alongside love, joy, peace, patience, kindness, goodness, gentleness, and self-control. Those qualities are not mere human virtues to be cultivated through sheer willpower but rather the natural outgrowth of a life rooted in God's love and nurtured by His Spirit.

Faithfulness, in its essence, is the quality of being steadfast, loyal, and true to one's commitments, especially in the face of adversity. When we speak of God's faithfulness, we refer to His unwavering commitment to His promises and people. That theme reverberates throughout the biblical narrative and continues to resonate in the lives of believers today.

The collection of stories herein is a testament to the many ways in which God's faithfulness manifests in human lives and how, in turn, human faithfulness to God bears fruit in the world. Each author brings a unique perspective… a personal encounter with the one and only True God who has shaped their understanding of faithfulness and its power to transform lives. Each story is an inspirational account and a practical guidepost for those seeking to develop faithfulness in their own lives.

One of the beautiful paradoxes explored in this collection of writings is the interplay between human and divine faithfulness. As each author shares their experience, a common theme emerges: the ability to remain faithful often stems from recognizing God's prior and present perfect faithfulness to us. In response to His unwavering love, we find the strength to persevere, trust, and remain loyal in our faith journey. Our faith grows stronger as we witness God's faithfulness in our lives. As our faith strengthens, we become more attuned to recognizing God's faithful acts, both subtle and grand. That heightened awareness deepens our trust and commitment, enabling us to remain steadfast despite life's most daunting challenges.

In an era often characterized by broken promises, fleeting commitments, and eroding trust, the stories in this book stand as a countercultural testament to the enduring power of faithfulness. They remind us that in a world of shifting sands, there is solid ground to be found in faith.

The authors of *God's Faithfulness Fruit* do not shy away from addressing the difficulties of maintaining faith in a sometimes hostile or indifferent society. Instead, they offer honest and transparent reflections on their struggles, doubts, and moments of weakness. It is through those vulnerable admissions that the true strength of faithfulness shines brightest, for faithfulness is not the absence of doubt but the persistence of trust in spite of it.

As you read the following accounts, you are invited to actively participate in the ongoing story of faith that will stand the test of time. Each narrative is a seed planted in the soil of your life experience, waiting to take root and bear sweet fruit. The authors' stories serve as both encouraging and challenging. They **encourage** us by demonstrating that faithfulness is possible, even in difficult circumstances. They **challenge** us to examine our own lives, identify areas where our faith may be weak, and recommit to the path of faithfulness.

One of the most powerful themes that emerges from this collection is the far-reaching impact of individual faithfulness. Like a stone cast into a pond, sending ripples across the surface, acts of faithfulness—no matter how small they may seem to others—have the potential to influence lives far beyond our immediate circle. Prepare to open your mind and heart to the journey ahead of you. Allow the experiences of these 17 authors to speak to you, challenge your presumptions, strengthen your determination, and deepen your perception of what it means to be faithful.

Remember: The Fruit of Faithfulness is not reserved for a select few, nor is it out of reach for those who seek it. Faithfulness is available to all who are willing to trust in God's promises, persevere through trials, and remain steadfast in their commitment to Him.

May the stories in *God's Faithfulness Fruit* nourish your spirit, strengthen your faith, and inspire you to cultivate the Fruit of Faithfulness in your own life. In a world hungry for authenticity, commitment, and enduring truth, let us together savor faithfulness' sweet fruit and, in doing so, become living testimonies to God's Faithfulness.

CORE SCRIPTURE

"… For truly, I say to you, if you have faith like a grain of mustard seed, you will say to this mountain, 'Move from here to there,' and it will move. Nothing will be impossible for you."
Matthew 17:20, ESV

MUSTARD-SEED FAITH – A POEM

Angela Edwards © 2024

In times of darkness, when hope seems lost,
Our faith in God becomes our light;
A beacon strong, no matter the cost,
Guiding us through the darkest night.

Through trials and tribulations we face,
Our spirits tested, our resolve tried,
We find within a wellspring of grace,
As in His love, we safely abide.

The storms may rage, the winds may blow,
Yet anchored firm in faith we stand.
For in our hearts, we surely know,
We're held secure in God's own hand.

Each challenge met, each hurdle cleared,
Builds strength within our very core.
The fears we've faced, the doubts we've neared,
Leave us much stronger than before.

Like gold refined in searing flame,
Our faith grows pure through every test;
Emerging brighter, free from blame,
In God's own image, truly blessed.

When burdens weigh, and sorrows press,
We turn our eyes to heaven above;
Finding solace in His gentleness,
Embraced by everlasting love.

The path may twist, the road may turn,
But faith propels us ever on.
Through hardships, vital lessons we learn,
Our spirits strengthened, doubts withdrawn.

In moments dark and moments bright,
God's presence never leaves our side.
His wisdom guides, His love our light,
In Him, we trust, in Him, abide.

As mountains moved by mustard seeds,
Our faith can conquer any fear.
Through actions bold and righteous deeds,
We draw to God's own purpose near.

So let us face each coming day,
With hearts uplifted, spirits strong.
For faith in God will light our way,
And fill our lives with joyous songs.

TABLE OF CONTENTS

DEDICATION	VI
ACKNOWLEDGMENTS	VII
FOREWORD	IX
INTRODUCTION	XII
CORE SCRIPTURE	XVI
MUSTARD-SEED FAITH – A POEM	XVII
ANGELA R. EDWARDS	1
By Faith, I Recovered It All	
MICKAYLA SAVAGE	8
God's Faithfulness Is More Than Enough	
REYNA HARRIS-GOYNES	14
Faith Is Inevitable	
MARLOWE R. SCOTT	19
The Fullness of Faith	
MARESA ROACH	27
Radical Recovery with Jesus Christ	
JOANNE B. LEWIS	36
It Was an Ordinary Day… Until It Wasn't	
SONYA MCKINZIE	45
Embracing My True Self	
QUIN LEVY	52
Tried and True	
FAITH MAKOWA	60
Cradled in Unwavering Promises	

ALLAINA MARIA 68
    Judas Was Me

MIN. JIMMY MERCHANT 75
    Job: The Faith-filled Man of God

KATINA RICE-DAVIS 81
    Anchored in Faith: A Journey Through Grief and Healing

GENAE KULAH 88
    Walking in Faith with the Pain of Reality
    In the Depths of Pain – A Poem

PRECIOUS DAMAS 96
    I Am Job

TOSHA R. DEARBONE 104
    God's Faithfulness Caused Me to Grow Up

LAURIE BENOIT 112
    The Pillars of Faithfulness: Loyalty, Trust, and Respect

JOURNAL YOUR FAITH WALK 122

ABOUT THE COMPILER 129

CONTACT THE PUBLISHER 132

ANGELA R. EDWARDS

Dedication: My story is dedicated to my mother, Marlowe R. Scott, for demonstrating all throughout my life what faith in God can do. I love you, Mom. Even when you may have thought I wasn't paying attention, I grasped the lessons. I pray I'm making you proud to be called "Mom."

Bio: Angela R. Edwards is a woman of God, wife, mother, and doting grandmother. Born and raised a "Jersey Girl," she currently resides in the Peach State of Georgia with her husband, James, and precious furbaby. She is the Owner of Pearly Gates Publishing and Redemption's Story Publishing and the Founder of the Battle-Scar Free Movement—a nonprofit that addresses domestic violence and abuse head-on while providing resources for victims and survivors to thrive after abuse. Angela loves life, loves to laugh, loves her family, and puts her faith into action at every turn. Her mantra is, *"Love life, and it will love you back!"*

By Faith, I Recovered It All

"But when you ask Him, be sure that your faith is in God alone. Do not waver, for a person with divided loyalty is as unsettled as a wave of the sea that is blown and tossed by the wind" (James 1:6, NLT).

How many people truly grasp the concept that there is a test in a testimony? It's not a pass/fail test, though. It's nothing like sitting in class, waiting for the teacher to hand out a piece of paper or booklet that they will "grade" afterward. Our progression to the next grade, phase, or level is often contingent upon passing a standardized test given to all those aspiring to leap forward right along with us.

Ohhhh, but there's something different—dare I say **"AMAZING?"**—about the test-turned-testimony experience that is unique to each of us and is largely dependent upon the lesson we need to learn to grow our faith.

As you read my faithfulness story, notice how exacting each lesson was. Admittedly, I gave the enemy plenty of ammunition to wreak havoc in my life, yet God never left me alone to fend for myself. My faith may have wavered a time or two during the tests, but my truths—my testimony—must be told. I share it with you in hopes that, should you find your own faith on unsteady ground, you will look to the heavens and cry out to the **ONLY ONE** who can save you… our Heavenly Father. I did, and I recovered it all!

****

For as long as I can remember, I have witnessed my mother exercising her faith muscles through various trials and tribulations. Mom Marlowe was a single mother to three (two boys and one girl). I watched as she prayed and called on God to provide every provision needed for her and her children. I was in awe many days and nights when God gave us food to eat when our cupboards were bare. I don't recall **EVER** going to bed hungry, even when I "just knew" we would. Mom has an active prayer life, believes in its power, and knows beyond a shadow of a doubt that her prayers **WILL** be answered. With over 50 years of experience under my belt, watching my mother uplift and empower others (including my two brothers and me) has blessed me with the precious gift of believing that God will show up and show out on my behalf—in His own time, of course.

It's important to note that God's timing is not ours. In fact, as I prepared to write this story, my faith muscles were stressed **OUT**. I recognized that it was **TEST TIME!** In all honesty, I'm still going through this very moment, but I know that God is faithful and just. He will never give any of us more than we can bear. Amen? Amen.

In the spirit realm, the devil hears us and sends his imps to destroy that very thing we speak aloud. Recently, I said something negative regarding struggling with my finances (OOPS!). No sooner than I spoke the words, I wanted to go into hiding because I knew the enemy was coming for me and would try to break my spirit. Sure enough, he came whispering, *"You don't deserve to prosper!"* Do you know that the devil is a **LIAR** and that there is no truth in him? I will not hide! I will not be held captive by the evil one! Just as my faith has always done, I'm choosing to hold steadfast to God's unchanging hand. This, too, shall pass!

I'm going to take you back to a time in my life when my choices led me to literally "lose it all." My wrong choices were the catalyst, so I knew I had to endure the spanking that was dished out. Although God was always with me during that tumultuous time, I didn't hear him when He said, *"STOP IT, ANGELA! STOP IT RIGHT NOW!"*

Many people know my domestic abuse survivor story. For those who don't, in a nutshell, my ex-husband was a narcissistic addict. Quite the combination, huh? Early in the marriage, I found myself enabling his behavior and addiction, even after he attempted to drag me down to the pits of Hell with him. I finally mustered up the strength to leave him after he tried to kill me and never looked back, but there was so much more to it than just a survivor story.

First and foremost, we were unequally yoked. I was raised in the Christian church; him, not so much. He had no solid footing on any particular religion outside of what was popularly known (at the time) as "Five-Percenters." Still, I fell in love, mesmerized by his ability to sway this good church girl to walk on the dirty side. To this day, I can't say I believe he ever loved me, but I can say with surety that the enemy of our souls had his sights set on me! Had I given in to the prompting of "my love" to ingest crack cocaine while being pinned down in the bathtub, where would I be? How would I have recovered, if at all?

Not long after our separation, I dated a couple of other guys who had similar traits as my now-ex, including them being addicted to some form of illegal narcotic. I just **KNEW** I hadn't learned whatever the lesson was because that quality of man just kept coming! ***"STOP IT, ANGELA!"***

At one point, the house I had owned since age 20, the car I purchased off the lot brand-new, and the government job I had worked hard to attain disappeared—a direct result of my bad choices. I looked around, dumbfounded by the severity of the losses and the vastness of emptiness, and wondered, *"What happened? Where did they go? What did I do so wrong to lose it all?"* My children (I had two before the marriage) and I were one pinky-toe shy of being homeless, **BUT GOD!** When I refocused my energy toward understanding the "why," I received a blunt yet gentle response from our Heavenly Father:

"You turned away from Me."

It was then that I realized I had, indeed, walked away from my first love. I will be among the first to say that life has its challenges. We were never told life would be easy. However, life is **SO** much more difficult when we know Christ for ourselves and then backslide our way into trials and tribulations that would likely not be as severe had we just listened and kept our faith in God. In fact, it was my faith that restored all that was lost—once I decided to let go and let God move in my life and not be tossed to and fro like the waves in a rough, stormy sea.

There's nothing quite like taking accountability for your wrongdoings. The redemptive power of the blood of Jesus Christ is not to be taken lightly or for granted.

"Then I acknowledged my sin to You and did not cover up my iniquity. I said, 'I will confess my transgressions to the LORD." And You forgave the guilt of my sin" (Psalm 32:5, NIV).

It took quite a few years to recover from the losses, even as other losses were presented. My pride had taken a hit.

Stability for the two children I was responsible for was at a crossroads, to the point that we moved in with my son's father (another ex) and his mother while we were in transition! Things got truly crazy out there while I clawed my way back to Jesus. Again, He never left me; it was I who was guilty of turning my back on Him. (Perhaps "clawed" is a tad bit extreme of a description, but that is what it felt like at the time.)

I recall my best friend of nearly 50 years, Marilyn, telling me she admired my faith. She was a witness to all the things I've mentioned here and more. She saw the tears and pierced her way through the smiles that often hid them. She walked the walk with me and saw me "in action" when recovery looked bleak, yet I managed to praise God anyhow. Here's the thing: It's not that Marilyn's own faith was weak or meant to be discounted. No. That's not why she professed admiration. She has her own story to tell, but I feel comfortable saying that more than anyone else in my circle at the time, she truly understood the challenges I was going through because of where she came from. She understood the struggle possibly more than I did because she had "been there, done that" at some point during her faith journey. I cannot overstate how much I appreciate her awareness of who I am.

I am honored to say that I see my children walking out their own walks of faith. Today, they have families of their own and are tasked with showing how God stands in the gap and fulfills our every need. I've watched both embrace God and not misstep haphazardly like I did. Although, as a parent, I did not want to traumatize my children, perhaps my journey was among the list of "Best Lessons Learned" for them, especially as they entered adulthood and grabbed life head-on. Hearing my daughter say from across the miles, *"I'm not worried. God got this!"* confirms she heard me say the same. Listening to my son share a recap of the Sunday sermon weekly warms my heart to the core. I'm grateful that God's Word never lies:

"Train up a child in the way he should go: and when he is old, he will not depart from it" (Proverbs 22:6, KJV).

God's faithfulness for His beloved children is tried and true. Every day we arise… every breath we take… every step we make is all because of His grace, mercy, and faithfulness toward each of us. I pause to think of where this world is headed. One day — perhaps one day very soon — those who love and accept Christ as their personal Savior will be caught up in the air with Him, heaven-bound to spend eternity fellowshipping with Him and the angels.

My sister- and brother-in-Christ, faith is not a one-time action; it is a lifestyle. For me, recovering it all was a process that took time, but I walked it out in faith. Always being mindful that there will be good and bad days, I implore you not to complain when things aren't going as you'd like. Rest in the test. Prepare for the testimony because it's coming. Lastly, be sure to tell somebody! Your testimony is for others! Amen? Amen! God Bless you, one and all!

MICKAYLA SAVAGE

Dedication: To our steadfast God, whose faithfulness sustains me through every trial. As a wife and mother to six precious children, I trust in His unwavering love and guidance. This journey of raising my family is filled with blessings and challenges, but His grace and strength make all things possible.

Bio: Mickayla Savage is a devoted wife and mother of six children in a beautifully blended family. She states, *"I have found unwavering strength in my faith. Each day presents new challenges and joys, but through it all, my trust in God's faithfulness guides me. His love has been my anchor, providing the wisdom and patience needed to nurture a family united in love. In every season of life, from the bustling chaos of daily routines to the quiet moments of reflection, I am reminded of His grace and provision. This journey, grounded in faith, is a testament to God's enduring presence in our lives."*

God's Faithfulness Is More Than Enough

Anytime I think about or am asked to share something about myself, I find it difficult. I am always unsure what moments or details of my life to share. It is almost like second-guessing who I am. For example, I started to write my faith story about notable struggles or victories I have faced in my lifetime, but the more I prayed, the more I heard a different message from God… a message to which I had never been receptive. What is that message, you ask? The answer is simple.

Deliver the message of God's faithfulness.

Writing about my faith is a lot like writing about a rollercoaster. For many years, I was raised in the "Bible Belt" region of the United States, where I was condemned for being… well, human. As such, the vast amount of my time exposed to religion or spent with religious people has felt nothing short of judgment and ridicule. I consistently felt like an outcast—a "not-good-enough Christian."

There have been numerous ups and downs regarding the measure of my faith in God, yet He remains. When I was on fire for the Lord, he was there. When I was living in unrepentant sin, He was there. Even when I questioned the very existence of our Savior, **HE WAS THERE!**

I ask that you, as my audience, forgive me in advance, as I may stumble through my words, and memories may run together. Please bear witness to my testimony and the grand scheme of the faithfulness of God.

****

When I speak to another person of faith or one who is at least open to understanding where my faith comes from, I prefer to mention references from the Holy Bible that relate to how I have overcome struggles in my life. I try not to dwell on the past because I cannot change it. The same goes for the future. For me, the first reminder of God's faithfulness is found in Jeremiah 29:11 (NIV): *"'For I know the plans I have for you,' declares the Lord, 'plans to prosper you and not to harm you, plans to give you hope and a future.'"*

As previously mentioned, my own faith has been like a rollercoaster of highs and lows. Years ago, I learned of a scripture that has stuck with me regarding the measure of faith: *"Because you have so little faith. Truly, I tell you, if you have faith as small as a mustard seed, you can say to this mountain, 'Move from here to there,' and it will move. Nothing will be impossible for you"* (Matthew 17:20, NIV). That passage simply means that no matter how big or how little, how strong or how questionable your faith in God may be, **it is enough.** It takes less than an ounce of faith for God to do miraculous things in our lives. Just like my testimony here, you don't need an elaborate prayer or a burning bush for God to show you how faithful He is. The only caveat to God's faithfulness, love, endurance, and grace is your acceptance.

Like a child who refuses to accept their parent's guidance, I have been guilty of refusing to accept the favor that God has had for me. There were moments when I thought God was calling me to do something, yet I convinced myself that I wasn't good enough or capable of doing what He intended, so I tried to run. I would make myself "too busy" to answer the call from God (something that still holds true for me today at times). All my life, I have wanted to be a mother. Even as a child, when asked what I wanted to be when I grew up, *"I'm going to be a mom!"* was my answer. Today, I have been blessed beyond measure with six children—yet I still run. I do busywork, such as trying to attend college and applying for jobs.

Mind you, I already have multiple degrees and a nursing license, so I could immediately go to work if necessary. My husband has an amazing career, and our household finances have been blessed, so I wouldn't need to find work at this time.

Amid it all, I find myself frustrated by not having the time I want to spend with my children because I am too busy running from my calling... the same one I prayed for that manifested at a young age... the same one God placed on my life! Just as I have prayed for the testimony I deliver to you now, I prayed for myself to accept the blessing and the calling that God has provided to me so that I can teach my children about the faithfulness of God, all while helping them grow in their own faith.

If there is one thing to take from this, it is that you cannot run, hide, outsmart, outdo, or outgrow God's calling on your life. His faithfulness will subdue your prerogative, and He will provide.

"...for God's gifts and His call are irrevocable" (Romans 11:29, NIV).

I pray that you will take my message and let it be one that can comfort you when you are going through your own walk of faith. I pray my words will help those in a place where they feel that their faith isn't enough or that they are unworthy of God's faithfulness. As it is said, *"It takes all kinds of kinds."* I believe that statement holds true in most scenarios, including our faith walk. There is no right or wrong way to be a Christian.

There is no right or wrong way to measure how much faith you do or don't have.

As for me, no one can convince me that God is looking down on me (or you), saying, *"You don't have as much faith today as you did one year ago. That might not be enough to get into Heaven."* Or *"You didn't earn My grace, mercy, love, or faithfulness today."* My God — **OUR GOD** — is a **trusting** God, a **loving** God, a **patient** God, and a **forgiving** God. He is faithful today, He was faithful yesterday, and He will be faithful tomorrow. Amen. The faithfulness that God provides is the certainty that regardless of our shortcomings, He is still the same God. Just as we lean on others for support here on earth when we are unsure or unstable, we can lean on and call on God and His faithfulness to see us through any trial we face.

Wherever you are, whoever you may be, please take your faith and let it grow… even if you only have faith the size of a mustard seed… even if you are unsure of God's calling on your life. If you have nothing else, have faith in the faithfulness of the Lord.

Lastly, before I go, I want to share a handwritten note my great-grandmother wrote in a book of poems two years before my birth. It was a testament to her faith and helped solidify my commitment to write my faith story in this publication.

"My philosophy of life is prayer and faith in God. I'm sure every day I make mistakes, but I always strive to do better tomorrow than I have today. Eleven years ago, I had heart surgery, and I was really scared then, but my faith wasn't very strong then, either. But with prayer and faith, I made it through.

"But now, I have a life-threatening problem. I've had surgery twice in the last four weeks, and real soon, God willing, I'll have my

third and final surgery. I have faith that everything is going to be alright, and if the news is bad, I know it's God's will, and I'll still have faith.

"So, prayer and faith is my philosophy of life."

Juanita Pillow
Philosophy

REYNA HARRIS-GOYNES

Dedication: My story is dedicated to my husband and kids. They motivate me to keep taking things one day at a time. I love you all. To my daughter Rey'Lynn: I love your outgoing, outspoken spirit. When people say, *"She's been here before,"* I believe them.

Bio: Reyna Harris-Goynes is a wife and mother of five. She is also a small business owner of V.R. Fashions & More and V.R. Mobile Notary. She is passionate about customizing items for her clientele. Throughout the years, she has also co-authored stories in multiple anthologies, including *God Says I am Battle-Scar Free* and the *God's Fruit* series. Reyna states, *"I love what I do, and I believe in my heart it's my purpose."*

Faith Is Inevitable

In January 2018, our lives were changed forever, but not as badly as we first thought. You see, my son Keyonte was diagnosed with Wilm's Tumor — *"a rare kidney cancer that affects children. It causes abdominal pain, swelling and mass in the abdomen, blood in urine, fever, nausea and vomiting, difficulty breathing, high blood pressure, loss of appetite, and constipation"* (Focus Medica, 2024). He was seven years old at the time of his diagnosis. I recall feeling as if we didn't know whether we were coming or going at any given moment. Who could we turn to in our desperate time of need? I'm grateful for my husband. Together, we pushed through, even while it felt like our backs were against the wall many days.

As time progressed, we learned to cope with the sudden change in our lives. As you might imagine, Keyonte's diagnosis was unexpected and traumatizing. Much like most other parents, we asked, *"Why did this happen to **our** son?"* After moving past our feelings of defeat and despondency, we realized there was nothing we could do other than support our son on his journey. Admittedly, it was challenging not to stress about the situation, but our faith in God assured us that He was always in control.

It seemed like almost everyone had turned their backs on us when we needed their support in a major way. When that happened, we knew God was showing us who was supposed to be on this journey with us. When He showed up and "removed people" from our lives, His choices were very interesting. Still, we made it through. My mom was there initially, but she eventually walked away, too. My husband and I were left to figure things out for ourselves, with the priority being getting our own vehicle to make the many trips to the hospital for Keyonte's treatments.

Running back and forth to the hospital for Keyonte's appointments added to the stress we endured, but he had to go—no matter what. Before long, the travel and cost to park became overwhelming, so I decided to stay at the facility overnight when he had treatments and other appointments. Throughout the course of time, the nurses and staff became like family to us, especially when we became "regulars," staying for three days or more at times.

During this experience, here's what I have learned: You can't expect you from others. People will sometimes unexpectedly turn on you after asking for some help, but that's not who I am. That's not what I do.

I also learned that no matter the outcome in life, I must always keep my faith in God. At the time of this writing, it's been 11 years since Keyonte's initial diagnosis, and it has always been our faith in God that has pulled us through to the other side. We are truly grateful to God, the hospital staff, and various children's foundations for keeping us positive and assuring us that Keyonte's cancer isn't our fault (that's what I believed for months after hearing the news). My husband also made sure I never gave up on our son.

Today, all I can say is, ***"BUT GOD!"*** Often, I've wanted to throw in the towel, but God threw it right back, saying, *"I'm not through with you yet! Keep the faith!"*

Forever Team Keyonte

****

Editor's Note:

A Journey of Faith: Finding Light in the Darkest Hours

As the sun rises one crisp autumn morning, I imagine the Goynes family standing hand-in-hand outside the hospital, their hearts filled with a mixture of gratitude and awe. Little Keyonte is now a vibrant and smiling teenager—a stark contrast to the frail child who entered the facility years ago. The family's journey through Keyonte's battle with Wilm's Tumor has been a crucible of faith, testing their beliefs, their relationships, and their very souls.

Looking back, Reyna could hardly believe the transformation she had undergone. The day of Keyonte's diagnosis felt like a lifetime ago—a moment frozen in time when her family's world had shattered into a thousand pieces. I can feel the cold fear that had likely gripped her heart and the overwhelming sense of hopelessness she faced against an enemy she couldn't see or understand.

When Reyna asked God, *"Why him?"* I could relate to that moment of raw vulnerability as her faith was being tested. Any earthly answer would seem hollow in the face of her son's suffering, but it was in that crucible of doubt that she found a deeper, more profound connection to her faith. She discovered that faith is not a passive waiting for things to get better. Reyna knew faith as an active force that propelled her forward, even on the days when moving forward seemed impossible.

From Reyna's story, I gleaned that her family learned faith doesn't shield us from life's hardships but provides a foundation to weather them. They also realized that faith isn't just a feeling; it's a choice that must be made daily. Whatever challenges lie ahead for them, let us pray collectively that her family will face them together. Clearly, their bonds have been strengthened by the fire they have walked through. Their faith is deeper, their love is stronger, and their hearts are more open to the mysteries of life and the power of unwavering faith in an Almighty God.

A pastor once said, *"Sometimes, faith isn't about having all the answers. It's about trusting in God, even when the path ahead is unclear."* I pray you allow those words to become a lifeline… a mantra you can cling to when the night seems darkest.

MARLOWE R. SCOTT

Dedication: To my parents, Carl and Helena Harris, who loved me and planted the love of Jesus Christ in my life and soul. To family, pastors, and church members who enriched my spiritual life. To Rev. Abie Kulynych, Pastor of City of Refuge Fellowship, who enriched me further by clarifying my spiritual gifts.

Bio: Marlowe Scott is 80 years old and an author who publishes inspirational books and stories through her daughter Angela R. Edwards' two publishing houses, Pearly Gates Publishing LLC and Redemption's Story Publishing LLC. Marlowe has written over a dozen inspirational books and participated in co-authoring the Fruit of the Spirit series as well as this Spiritual Warfare series. Her books have earned awards, including #1 Bestseller, International Bestseller, and Hot New Release. One of her favorite songs is *"When I Think of the Goodness of Jesus and All He's Done for Me, My Soul Cries Out Hallelujah! I Thank God for Saving ME!"*

The Fullness of Faith

Introduction:

The following well-known hymn written by Thomas Chisholm (1866-1960) and music composed by William M. Runyan (1870-1957) is based on Lamentations 3:22-23: *"It is of the LORD's mercies that we are not consumed, because His compassions fail not. They are new every morning: great is Thy faithfulness."*

"Great Is Thy Faithfulness"

Verse 1: Great is thy faithfulness; O God, my Father,
There is no shadow of turning with Thee;
Thou changest not, Thy compassions, they fail not.
As Thou hast been, Thou forever wilt be.

CHORUS: Great is Thy faithfulness! Great is Thy faithfulness!
Morning by morning, new mercies I see;
All that I have needed, Thy hand hath provided.
Great is Thy faithfulness, Lord, unto me!

Verse 2: Summer and winter, and springtime and harvest;
Sun, moon, and stars in their courses above,
Join with all nature in manifold witness
To Thy great faithfulness, mercy, and love.

Verse 3: Pardon for sin and a peace that endureth,
Thine own dear presence to cheer and to guide;
Strength for today and bright hope for tomorrow,
Blessings all mine, with ten thousand beside!

Author's note: In writing my story, the confirmations found in the hymn will be shared.

Theme Text: Psalm 86:15

"But you, O Lord, are a God merciful and gracious, slow to anger and abounding in steadfast love and faithfulness" (ESV).

"But you, O Lord, are a God of compassion and mercy, slow to get angry and filled with unfailing love and faithfulness" (NLT).

****

When God created Heaven and Earth, He made sure we were given everything every one of us would need. In my life, I have found that to be true. There is food, water, protection, the ability to reproduce, and He is ever-present. The Fruit of The Holy Spirit became evident at the baptism of Jesus and is still with His people today who believe in Him.

In thinking of things people experience today, I am drawn to a centuries-old water geyser named "Old Faithful." It's important to note that the large hot water source it spews high in the air is from a volcano deep in the earth! We often think of a volcano as spewing fire and molten chunks of soil and rocks, destroying everything on its path, including people, villages, animals, etc. Even while this story was being written, one of the smaller areas erupted, spewing soil, rock, and fire with people nearby, destroying the boardwalk, benches, and areas around it.

You may be thinking, *"What does that have to do with faithfulness?"* The answer is not hard to understand. The Old Faithful geyser made me think of how, on the last day on earth, the Holy Bible says that the dead in Jesus Christ shall rise, and there will be a great sound. Afterward, those who believe will be caught up to meet our Savior in the sky! Those who don't believe in Him will be thrown into a lake of fire — **HELL** — for all eternity!

The characteristics of our loving God are:
- Loving
- Trustworthy
- Unchanging
- Steadfast
- Patient
- Committed
- Firm
- Offering Security

Fidelity is a characteristic He expects His people to display in their earthly moral life and interactions (moral = a person's standards of behavior or beliefs concerning what is and is not acceptable for them to do). Yes, God offers forgiveness, but that is not a license to keep doing and thinking wrong and acting in ways He would not have us do.

Simplifying faithfulness is easy for me because of my experiences throughout the 80 years of my life, which are rooted in the blessing of being born and raised in a Christ-centered home. I cannot recall when I first realized I knew who Jesus was, but I know it was when I was a child. My family attended church every Sunday. My parents read devotions daily, and I learned children's songs like "Jesus Loves Me" and "Jesus Loved All the Children of the World." The seeds of God's love were planted early in me by my family and church family. As I got older, through Sunday School, Bible study, and church attendance, I learned the hymn "Great Is Thy Faithfulness" and each Fruit of the Spirit (although I didn't fully understand each one). In the natural, the only thing I knew about fruit was that it was something good to eat, cook, and preserve. Those same characteristics and more apply to the Fruit of the Spirit!

I have known women named Faith. The name has been popular since the 17th century and means "trust or devotion." In ancient times, parents gave their daughters that name to symbolize hope for the child, that she would have a strong religious foundation and steadfast beliefs. In today's world, many children are given names with meanings that steer far from a spiritual foundation.

While I believe that former sentence to be accurate, the depth and fullness of the Spiritual Fruit names are **AWESOME, COMFORTING, OFFER PROTECTION,** continued **LOVE**, plus much more. There is no match for it because *GOD* sent the Holy Spirit in the form of a dove when Jesus Christ was baptized by John the Baptist with the Fruit of the Spirit. The Holy Spirit is active and remains with us until Jesus returns on the last day the earth as we know it is gone.

What I have personally received by the faithfulness of the Holy Spirit that lives in my soul:
- Love
- Protection
- Peace
- Grace

In writing this story, I broke the word "Faithfulness" into three parts. Those thoughts put me in mind of the Trinity (God, Holy Spirit, Jesus — three in One).

Faith – belief in the unchangeable love of God and Jesus.

Ful – adds to our life, well-being, and protection.

Ness – always there, unchanging. (As this word can be a noun in some ways, in other languages, it means 'a very large piece of land sticking out into the sea; a headland or point. It is a narrow piece of land that projects from a coastline into the sea; a strip of land left unplowed at the end of a field.')

I equate and simplify all the above to mean that faithfulness unites people and things. Think about Jonah and the whale. He was put overboard, but God had a whale swallow him until he could be spewed out onto dry land. Another instance is when Peter walked on the water toward Jesus. He began to sink, but Jesus stretched out His hand to him, and he was saved. There are times when God reaches down and saves us, so we must give credit where credit is due.

As I was writing, I was blessed with the following two statements from my daily devotional by Dr. Charles Stanley, who is now deceased:

"Though we'll never grasp the infinite mind of God, we can know His faithfulness and love." (7/16/24)

"Trials are an opportunity to experience our heavenly Father's faithfulness and strength." (7/17/24)

Another hymn that excites me and confirms spiritual love is *"My Faith Looks Up to Thee,"* written by Ray Palmer, who was born in Little Compton, Rhode Island, in 1808 and died in Newark, New Jersey, in 1887.

Verse 1: *May faith looks up to Thee, thou Lamb of Calvary, Savior divine!*
Now, hear me while I pray: take all my guilt away.
O, let me, from this day, be wholly Thine!

Verse 2: *May Thy rich grace impart strength to my fainting heart, my zeal inspire!*

	As Thou hast died for me, O may my love to Thee,
	Pure, warm, and changeless, be a living fire.
Verse 3:	*While life's dark maze I tread, and griefs around me spread,*
	Be Thou my guide; bid darkness turn to day, wipe sorrow's tears away,
	Nor let me ever stray from Thee aside.
Verse 4:	*When ends life's transient dream, when death's cold, sullen stream*
	Shall o'er me roll; blest Savior, then in love, fear, and distrust remove;
	O, bear me safe above, a ransomed soul!

Conclusion:

In my biography, I mentioned Rev. Abie Kulynych, Pastor of City of Refuge Fellowship in Burlington, New Jersey. His impact on my life is a blessing, **PLUS** so much more! He was able to understand me and my Spiritual Gifts clearly, and he is gifted with great depth of understanding while explaining the scriptures.

On the 1st day of August 2024, I read one of his weekly social media posts. My soul leaped when I saw the following words:

"The cure for discouragement is faithfulness."

That was yet another message and confirmation that God and the Holy Spirit are always with me, fulfilling my every need. Just to share more of Rev. Kulynych's post, he wrote:

"…it's being faithful to my relationship to Him, trusting His goodness when I don't see it, His love when I don't feel it, His Word when I don't understand it. It's being obedient to what I know rather than trying to grab something new that might get a better or faster

result…" There was more, but the conclusion is, "I know it may sound a bit too simple, but I've tested it over and over again, and I've learned that the cure for discouragement really is faithfulness."

Final Thought…

After completing this story, another spiritual experience occurred, demonstrating how the Holy Spirit was working inside of me. A long-time Christian friend stayed on my mind, and I didn't know why. Then, my daughter, who creates one-of-a-kind personalized gifts, made a beautiful pillow cover with 1 Thessalonians 5:17 printed on it with a bouquet of flowers. The simple word "PRAY" was printed in large letters. Over the years, I have prayed with and for my friend. We share how many denominations and Christians are drifting toward worldliness and copying worldly ways. **WE PRAY!**

While waiting for my time to be joined with Jesus in the heavens, I am thankful for **GOD'S FAITHFULNESS** through the years!

MARESA ROACH

Dedication: My story is dedicated to those suffering from substance abuse disorders, mental health issues, and adverse childhood experiences. It's never too late to follow your dreams. Believe in yourself, and remember: Failure is **NOT** an option! Delayed is not denied! Your mistakes and challenges do not determine who God says you are.

Bio: Maresa Roach has an infectious smile, a bubbly personality, and a welcoming presence that can light up any room! You would likely not be able to tell that her past was a series of painful experiences laden with disappointment and despair. As a youngster, she was very shy with low self-esteem. By the age of 15, she'd suffered from trauma. It seemed as if self-doubt and shame would win in her life, but **GOD** had a much larger plan—one that turned her past *"SHAME INTO SHINE"* to be a blessing in the lives of others!

Radical Recovery with Jesus Christ

In this saga, you will read about patterns of self-destruction, self-harm, low self-worth, and challenges I endured due to childhood trauma. But through recovery, I found peace. Dictionary.com defines recovery as *"to get back, to make up for, to regain the strength, composure, or balance of, to reclaim."* Recovery gave me the needed time to regain my balance… balance within my relationship with God and myself. I slowly allowed God to put my life back together.

During 2020, I was depressed and suffered from anxiety. I was not eating or sleeping, all while grieving from a break-up and drinking alcohol nearly every day to fill my empty soul. Although I grew up in the church and got saved as a little girl, I'd not been living a Christian lifestyle, nor was my relationship with Jesus Christ strong. I had an on-again, off-again walk with the Lord. At the time, I was "living my best life," albeit a life of sin, fornication, alcoholism, partying, and just outright ratchetness. I rarely paused to consider the repercussions of my sinful lifestyle.

What I do know is this: I had a reprobated mind. I had turned my back on God because I thought **HE** turned **HIS** back on me. I believed I was cursed, openly expressing to my mother, *"God has cursed me for all the sins I have committed."* Everything that could've happened wrong in my life seemed to happen.

Childhood Background

I grew up in a single-parent home with my mother and sister. When I was two years old, we moved from Lorain, Ohio, to Washington, D.C. My mother was young and taught my sister and me how to live clean and holy lives. Although we lived in the "hood," my mom did her best to keep us off the streets and in the house. There were no drugs or alcohol in our home (at least, not that I knew of). My mother didn't curse, drink, or smoke.

What I didn't know until later in life was that my father was an alcoholic. He was murdered in a bar by a white man while I was in my mom's womb. My mother didn't talk about my father until my later years. Those conversations, coupled with the ones we have now, explain some of our upbringing and why I share some of my father's characteristics.

I have often wondered how my life would've turned out if my father was alive. I wonder if my daddy would've been in my life to protect me from the bullies I encountered in school and in the world. *Would he have been there when I needed someone to talk to about relationships with boys/men? Would he have helped me find my way in life? Would he have been there for me at all?* If so, perhaps I would have made better decisions with men and in my life.

History of Substance Use

In my 20s, I was introduced to crack cocaine. A guy I was hanging out with introduced it to me through an older couple he smoked with. (That same guy died by the hand of that awful substance.) Roughly four years later, God saved me from that addiction. I visited my grandmother and stayed with her for about two weeks. During that time, I went cold turkey without the aid of any other substances. No Newport 100 cigarettes. No alcoholic beverages. No marijuana. And, most importantly, no crack cocaine. God healed me within a matter of weeks. **HE** released me from those substances.

In 1991, I no longer desired to use any toxic substances. I was clean, free, and delivered! From 1991 until 1996, I did not drink or smoke. What I don't remember was gaining a clean slate with Jesus Christ. As I type this, I realize that although I was clean of all those harmful substances, I hadn't gained a clean walk with God. My heart wasn't renewed. (That is the root of what you'll read about in the following few paragraphs.)

There was a period in 2009 when I resumed consuming alcohol. I didn't smoke, but drinking and partying were my "thing." I thought addiction was a thing of the past, but what I didn't know was that it was in my bloodline... a generational curse... a stronghold. The childhood trauma and unresolved issues remained with me. I had no idea that not ever seeing my father (grief and loss), losing my virginity at age 15, a sexual assault, and intimate partner violence (domestic abuse) had taken a toll on my life internally, all because I hadn't used the tools in my toolbox: Jesus and therapy.

School Days

Fast-forward to 2017, when I was accepted into Howard University School of Social Work (HUSSW). I made it through the first year successfully but struggled through the second year. A concerned friend called me one day because I often disappeared, did not call anyone, and did not check in. I just slept and wouldn't eat for days at a time. I didn't want to answer the phone but did so eventually. My friend asked me to send him a picture of my insurance card. In response, he sent me a list of ten therapists.

In my hungover stooper, I called each therapist and left a message. The tenth therapist returned my call, and we began the intake process. After the intake and two sessions, I asked, *"What's my diagnosis?"*

She stated, *"Your diagnosis is Generalized Anxiety and Major Depression due to your current challenges with school and unresolved trauma responses."*

My studies began to suffer. As a social work student, I was unable to commit items to memory when studying and was challenged with recall. I asked my therapist to have an IQ and other testing done to get to the root of my problem. Some of the issues were due to adverse trauma I hadn't addressed. I had panic and anxiety attacks (in and outside of class), I feared school assignments and the professors, and I didn't believe I was worthy as a student.

The trauma from the past haunted me. At an early age, I was sexually assaulted, abused, and introduced to drugs and alcohol. The 15-year-old little girl in me had not dealt with her self-image, low self-esteem, and unforgiveness for herself and others. I had so many things bottled up inside. They needed to be released from the bottle. Otherwise, I would have exploded! I used alcohol as a conduit to ease the pain and suffering I endured on the inside. I must admit: **I was afraid.** Afraid of school. Afraid of failing. Afraid of the work. Afraid of speaking up. Afraid of answering questions, raising my hand, and committing to the test. I was just downright afraid. All that people had told me throughout the years, I believed and began to doubt myself.

In therapy sessions that followed, I would often declare, *"I am no good for myself or others."* It was reminiscent of times in my life when I would sit on the floor of my apartment and contemplate committing suicide, saying to myself, *"I am no good. I hadn't fulfilled any of my dreams. No one would miss me."*

Ohhhhh, BUT GOD! He's had His hand on me since the beginning of time!

Dream Deferred

I was roughly five weeks away from obtaining a Master of Social Work degree but withdrew. I was not ready. I was a hot mess. The stressors of financial obligations, finals, pop quizzes, group presentations, research papers, and the loss of one of my favorite professors had me in a chokehold. I was stressed and chose to self-medicate to deal with all the pressure. No matter what I did, I could not seem to find my way back.

That behavior was reminiscent of the past before I registered for graduate school. I'd gone through a spell of grief and the loss of several loved ones after graduating from The University of the District of Columbia, where I earned a Bachelor of Social Work. At the time, I put my dream of enrolling in HUSSW on hold. It seemed I had adopted a pattern of quitting.

There Had to Be Another Way

I struggled with an addiction to alcohol until almost three years ago. From ages 15 to 54, I drank alcohol on and off again. As mentioned earlier, graduate school, the stressors of life, research papers, finances, my living situation, toxic relationships, and a little bit of peer pressure (my colleagues loved to go to 'Happy Hour') were conduits of my drinking. My colleagues weren't aware of my drinking problem until later up the road. I found myself dealing with what I felt was the worst go-round ever.

I was so ashamed of my drinking that I would hide the cans and bottles in my room, pile them up, put them in a bag, and throw them in the dumpster when I thought no one was around to see the many bags. I self-soothed, hoping to drown the feelings of pain and loss. I knew there had to be another way out of this life of alcoholism.

Test Became a Testimonial

I gave the depression and anxiety to God in 2020. After giving my stressors to God, I developed a closer walk with Him. I joined the Outreach ministry at the previous church I attended. I evangelized, read my Word, prayed, fasted, and surrendered my stressors to Jesus Christ. I knew why I had to withdraw from the school of social work. If I continued the lifestyle I was living—drinking and stewing in depression—I would not have the relationship or testimony I have today. I am working in my purpose.

After surrendering the depression and anxiety to God, I stopped drinking for a while but would still go out with friends and have a glass of wine here and there or everywhere. The history of alcoholism in my bloodline played a major role in my mental, physical, and spiritual health. Alcoholism, like any disease, is an illness. I wasn't openly honest with myself. Those around me didn't know how to address my sickness, and, quite frankly, I wish they had. I was crying out for help silently.

Finally, in November 2022, I decided I would no longer drink. In January 2023, I completely gave up the desire during my church's annual 21-day Fast. As I gave up drinking, I journaled and participated in a book collaboration titled *Faith for Fiery Trials, Volume III*, where we became Amazon #1 Bestselling Authors. I also began to post my testimonials on Facebook Live and attended the Woman Evolve Conference 2023, where I surrendered all hope to God. I got baptized on January 27, 2024, and have been a featured guest on podcast interviews, blogs, and e-magazines. I've written two books and one devotional and shared my testimony at a Women's Conference.

My recovery from living a life of sin, alcoholism, major depression, and suicidal ideation deems me the perfect candidate to share the gospel of Jesus Christ. I use my platform to let people know they don't have to come home (to the church) perfect and flawless. We all fall short of God's glory.
For many years, I ran away from God. I wasn't ready to fully surrender my life to Him. I have since been redeemed through His blood. I radically changed my life of sin, shame, and dysfunction by surrendering it all to Jesus Christ! I am at peace and have found recovery with Jesus! I am free of the disease because I turned it over to Him!

"Some trust in chariots and some in horses, but we trust in the name of the LORD our God. They are brought to their knees and fall, but we rise up and stand firm" (Psalm 20:7-8, NIV).

You are encouraged to use the following resources to help you on your journey to healing:

- National Council for Mental Well-Being
  www.thenationalcouncil.org
- Better Help
  www.betterhelp.com
- Psychology Today
  www.psychologytoday.com
- Suicide Prevention – If you or someone you know is in crisis, contact the Suicide Prevention Lifeline at: 1-800-273-TALK (8255) or dial 911 in case of an emergency.
- Sexual Assault/Rape
  Rape, Abuse & Incest National Network (RAINN)
  www.rainn.org
- National Sexual Assault Hotline
  1-800-656-4673
- Domestic Violence
  www.domesticviolence.org

You are also welcome to contact me directly:
On the web at www.maresacoach.com or via email at maresatheauthor149@gmail.com.

JOANNE B. LEWIS

Dedication: To my husband, family, ancestors, and my angels, my mother, Armielee Hughley Ballard, my sweet sister-in-luv, my Tina. I will forever feel the love from all of you. I am full of dreams that are coming to fruition. I thank You, Lord. I know I. AM. Enough.

Bio: Joanne B. Lewis is a retired Ohio Licensed Social Worker and educator, 3x bestselling author, advocate for all people living their best life, and a tireless advocate for women and their families. As the Founder/CEO owner of Hope For Today, LLC, a non-profit organization established in 2023 to bring awareness to bringing inspiration to people. Joanne is a member of Alpha Kappa Alpha Sorority, Inc. Connect with her on the web at iamjoanneblewis1.com or via email at jblewis1908@yahoo.com.

It Was an Ordinary Day. Until It Wasn't

It started out as a great day. I was excited and on my way to speak to a group of students at the local college. I was dressed for success and prepared to deliver a great presentation.

Seattle traffic has a notorious history of backups and never-ending traffic. I glanced in my rearview mirror and saw a woman driver talking on her phone. The next thing I knew, I was rear-ended with such force that I felt my head and neck hit the headrest back and forth violently. After the car came to a stop, I felt as if my brain was moving around in my head. The inside of my head felt "mushy." That is the best way I can describe what I was feeling. The pain was severe and indescribable. I tried my best to collect myself, but the mushy, disoriented feeling would not subside. I was nauseated due to the unrelenting pain.

I wondered if the woman who hit me was going to exit her car and come to see if I was okay. I waited and waited. She finally approached my car, and her first words were, *"Traffic is terrible!"* I looked at her dazed, trying to understand if she had really said that to me. At no time did she ask, **"Are you okay?"** The arrogance, privilege, and entitlement she displayed was disconcerting. She had absolutely no regard for my brown body and wellbeing. Her next words to me were, *"We should move the cars over so that we don't block traffic."*

"What?!" I thought. I quickly told her I was not moving my car anywhere and did not care about "blocking the traffic." She inquired if I called the police, to which I replied, *"Of course*

I did! You hit me!" She returned to her car, and we both waited for the police to come to the accident scene.

****

That day started out as an ordinary day… until it wasn't. In fact, it was the start of a new season in my life—a season where I would learn to lean into Romans 8:26 (NIV): *"In the same way, the Spirit helps us in our weakness. We do not know what we ought to pray for, but the Spirit Himself intercedes for us through wordless groans."* That scripture has been my comfort in my darkest times. I have learned and come to know that God's words are always true.

I was afraid that something terrible had happened in my head and had many questions. Why was the inside of my head feeling mushy? What was this pain? I could hardly keep my eyes open. The daylight hurt my eyes, and my neck felt like it was on fire.

The initial emergency room visit was the start of an indescribable journey, one that would lead me to what seemed like a dark and never-ending road. During that visit, I received an MRI (a noninvasive medical imagining technique) of my head and neck and was given medication for nausea and pain. The MRI showed no initial concerns. I was told that after a car accident, it might take a couple of days before I started to feel better.

A few days passed, and I still had an unrelenting headache that would not end. I scheduled an appointment to see my primary physician. During that visit, I was told that everything seemed normal and that I should be able to do the things I was doing prior to the accident. I explained to her that

I was still experiencing pain in my neck and head. I felt so unseen and not taken seriously. My words of pain were falling on deaf ears. I remember during one of the appointments, she looked at me as if to say, *"You're not **really** in any pain."* I felt I did not matter and that she did not believe me. From that first visit with my primary doctor and throughout the appointments that followed with other doctors, my head continued to hurt. The pain would not stop!

During the course of this journey, I had bloodwork, X-rays of my head and neck, MRIs, CAT scans, and more, all to try and determine what was causing such severe pain and other issues I was experiencing. Test after test, I received the same results: There was no damage seen that would explain my head pain, stuttering, the change in function to my left foot, loss of taste and smell, and my inability to write or read.

Something was different about the pain in my head, though. There was not a moment during the day or evening when I did not feel excruciating pain. I had to stop driving because it was too confusing and upsetting. My husband and my sweet Sista-Neighbor drove me to my appointments. One day, I told my Sista-Neighbor that I was going to drive myself to the hospital because I was in so much pain. She replied, **"No, you are not!"** That day, she left her job to take care of me and drive me to the hospital. I'm also grateful for my church family, who prayed for me continuously.

I tried my best to move past the pain by doing all the things I would have normally done throughout the day, but the pain was still there. I could not do anything. The pain affected every aspect of my life. I could not eat very much because I felt nauseous. I was prescribed medications for nausea and pain. I eventually stopped taking both because neither helped. I swiftly fell into a depression. My days consisted of waking up, feeling sick, and being in pain with the same headache. Showering and getting dressed took too much energy. I would grab a blanket and climb into my chair, which became my daily routine. I was in pain and depressed every day.

I explained to the doctor that I had lost my sense of taste and smell. Everything I ate tasted like nothing. If I smelled perfume, food, or flowers, I could not smell a thing. She stated that she had never heard of that being a result of a car accident. I also told her my ability to read was gone. When I tried, I could not comprehend what I read, and the words appeared on the page looking like a jumbled word puzzle. I could not read anything, not even my Bible. My ability to write even the simplest word was a challenge as well. I could not do it. I recall trying to write the word "and," but I could not figure out how to write or spell it. That was so upsetting to me. After all, I had a master's degree! I knew how to write, yet I could not accomplish the task.

To add to my maladies and frustrations, I began to stutter. I had never stuttered before in my life. When I wanted to speak, I could feel an uncomfortable vibration on the back of my tongue (to this day, I still stutter). I would immediately apologize and sometimes cry. *"Why did this happen? What was wrong with me?"* I would ask myself. My sister would tell me, *"Stop apologizing."* My beloved husband would say to me over and over that I never had to apologize, and he would hug me until I stopped crying. Our children would say, *"Mom, you don't need to apologize."* My gait changed on my left side as well. While walking, my foot would drag. Trying to walk normally was truly tough.

My primary doctor looked at me with an unconcerned look and informed me she would refer me to see a psychiatrist, speech therapist, physical therapist, neurologist, acupuncturist, Otolaryngologist, and pain management specialist. I was so upset about her actually thinking I needed to see a psychiatrist. Did she not believe me? I was experiencing real pain! Of all the times I saw her for my pain, not once did she ever say, *"I am sorry this happened to you."* She never asked me, *"How are you feeling?"* **Where was her empathy?!** (I did not think about changing to a different primary care physician at the time.)

First, I saw the psychiatrist. He was a very pompous and condescending man. When he asked if there was anything I could do to lessen the pain in my head, I told him no. I described the pain in my head, the medications I had been prescribed, and the outcome of those medications. He replied, *"Based on my professional opinion, you should not have that kind of pain. After all, it was just a rear-end accident."* He wrote a new prescription, handed it to me, and said, *"This should help."* I left his office feeling frustrated, upset, unseen, and unheard. I tore up the prescription. I know that was not what I needed.

The neurologist ordered an MRI and CAT scan of my head. Those tests all came back "normal." One visit with the speech therapist found no abnormalities. I visited the physical therapist, who gave me exercises for my leg and foot to do while at home. I had biweekly visits over the course of a couple of months with the acupuncturist, who placed 80+ needles in key areas of my body to unblock nerve channels. Of all the visits, the one with the Otolaryngologist was the most encouraging. After completing the taste and smell tests, the doctor acknowledged that I, indeed, had no taste or smell. I finally felt heard, seen, and believed! I learned my loss of taste and smell was directly related to the trauma from the car accident.

I began to research "head pain after automobile accidents" and learned that the head pain I had been experiencing for months was called TBI—Traumatic Brain Injury. TBI can last for months, years, or a lifetime. I then contacted the medical records department at each provider I saw to request a summary of the actual notes each made regarding my case. Well, to my surprise, after reviewing the notes from the psychiatrist, he had noted in his summary that I had sustained a TBI! *"What?!"* I thought. *"Traumatic Brain Injury! Why in the world did he not tell me that? Was this information given to the other providers? And if not, why? And if so, why didn't any provider tell me?"*

Unseen. Unheard. Not taken seriously. Invisible. Yes, I felt **invisible**. I was furious but then decided I did not have time to be angry because I was still experiencing debilitating pain.

I was referred to a pain management doctor for my chronic pain. That doctor advised that the best course of treatment would be a guided needle Occipital nerve block. The procedure was explained, and I thought I fully understood. I was then ushered into a sterile procedure room where there was a nurse, anesthetist, radiologist, and doctor. I laid face-down on an operating table and was given an IV with fluids and medication to numb the area at the base of my head. I felt the pain and shock of the needle trying to go into the back of my head. I said, *"It is too painful!"* More numbing medication was placed into the IV. The procedure was terrifying. The numbing medication was not effective whatsoever. I was encouraged to try to be still and slow my breathing. I did my best, but it was still too much. I told them to stop. I asked about being sedated instead and was told sedation would not benefit the procedure because I needed to be awake and relaxed. *"I'm definitely awake, but I'm nowhere near relaxed!"* I stated.

I underwent the procedure two more times. No amount of numbing medication worked. The third time was the absolute worst. The pain was reverting and shook me to my core. I felt like I was an experiment in a laboratory, just to see how much pain I could tolerate. My wrists and ankles were strapped down, so I could not move. I was being violated with no concern for the level of pain I was in. I cried out, ***"Stop! Stop! I cannot do this anymore!"*** After they released my wrists and ankles, I told them, *"I will **never** endure that again!"*

I felt so broken… so *invisible*. My thoughts veered to my ancestors. Is that what it was like for them, being strapped down and feeling inconceivable pain?

I left that procedure room, crying so hard. I was visibly upset and shaking. My husband ran over to me, asking what happened. He held me tightly. I was inconsolable. Someone in the room handed me water and a Kleenex. My husband sat me down and continued to embrace me. I could not speak for a few minutes. When I gathered myself enough to talk, I told him what happened to me and explained the excruciating pain I had endured. At that moment, all I really wanted was my mother. She's with Jesus, yet I knew she was with me. I wanted to talk to my sister. I knew she would hear me. I told my husband, *"I had promised Jesus that if He wanted me to live with this headache the rest of my life, then I would not complain and would give Him the glory. I will **NEVER** allow any type of procedure like that to happen to my body again!"* He went to find a doctor to discuss what happened in that procedure room. After a while, he returned and then drove me home.

****

That day is seared into my head and heart, as is my promise to Jesus. Every day, I continued to confess my love for Jesus and would tell anyone who would listen about the vow I made to Him.

The headache continued… until it did not.

I woke up one morning and felt a surge go through my body. That very moment, the headache was gone! And to this day, I have not suffered another headache. That was the day I woke up expecting the same pain until it was not the same. That day became my new "Ordinary Day." I dismissed the primary doctor and wrote a letter to the head of the hospital about the lack of bedside manner and professionalism.

During that dark journey, I remembered that the Holy Spirit would cover me in prayer when I could not pray for myself. God is my strength each and every day, and I cannot begin to thank Him enough.

SONYA MCKINZIE

Dedication: To my mother, Barbara Green, whose unwavering love and wisdom have guided me through life, and to my daughter, McKinzie Baker, whose boundless energy and joy inspire me every day. This chapter is a testament to our strength and the love that binds our family together.

Bio: Dr. Sonya Alise McKinzie is a Senior Client Success Leader with Ricoh USA. She is also a certified Trauma and Recovery Life Coach and has been honored with a Proclamation for ThriveHER Day in Brunswick, Georgia. She received an honorary doctorate in Humanitarianism and is a 2024 Presidential Lifetime Achievement Award recipient. She is also a #1 Amazon Bestselling Author in numerous categories, has written and contributed to over 25 books, and is the Visionary Author for the recently released Amazon Bestseller *Blueprint of a ThriveHER* anthology. Dr. Sonya loves empowering individuals to create HUGE footprints that will make a positive mark on the lives of others!

Embracing My True Self

When I was 13 years old, I remember looking in the mirror and hating the reflection staring back at me. I was tall, awkward, and dark-skinned, with extremely full lips and a large forehead. I was often picked on and ridiculed for my dark skin, broad body, and prominent forehead. For decades, I felt the need to self-sabotage because no one could see me as anything more than an unattractive black girl. When I turned 21, I realized that the color of my skin was one that was often looked down upon in the light but envied in the dark.

As the years passed, I gradually realized that my value was not tethered to the limited and often harsh judgments of others. The path to self-acceptance was challenging and filled with moments of doubt and introspection, but it was ultimately a journey of profound change. Each step forward was a small victory as I learned to quiet the negative voices that had long overshadowed my sense of self. With the support of those who truly saw and appreciated me, I began to recognize my unique attributes as sources of strength rather than imperfections.

However, the transformation was not instantaneous; it was a slow and steady process, much like a flower blooming after a long winter. Through the journey, I discovered true worth is found within, and embracing my authentic self became the most empowering act of love I could give myself.

"I praise You because I am fearfully and wonderfully made; Your works are wonderful, I know that full well" (Psalm 139:14, NIV).

At 21, a pivotal moment occurred that changed my perception of myself forever.

I had spent years feeling ashamed of my dark skin, high cheekbones, full lips, and unique features, believing they were flaws that set me apart in a negative way. But one evening, as I stood in front of the mirror, something shifted. I began to trace the contours of my face with my fingers, examining each feature with a newfound curiosity.

"For we are God's handiwork, created in Christ Jesus to do good works, which God prepared in advance for us to do" (Ephesians 2:10, NIV).

For the first time, I didn't see any flaws. Instead, I saw a story of strength and survival etched into my skin. My dark complexion—once a source of shame—now appeared as a beautiful canvas painted with the hues of my ancestors. Each shade told a tale of endurance and spirit, a testament to the rich history and heritage that I was a part of.

"But the Lord said to Samuel, 'Do not consider his appearance or his height, for I have rejected him. The Lord does not look at the things people look at. People look at the outward appearance, but the Lord looks at the heart'" (1 Samuel 16:7, NIV).

That realization didn't happen overnight. It was a gradual process sparked by small moments of self-discovery and reflection. I started to see the beauty in my dark skin, full lips, and unique features. I realized the very traits I had been mocked for were the same ones that made me stand out in a crowd. Once a source of shame, my skin became a symbol of resilience and strength. I began to embrace my heritage and the rich history that came with it.

"Consider it pure joy, my brothers and sisters, whenever you face trials of many kinds, because you know that the testing of your faith produces perseverance" (James 1:2-3, NIV).

As I continued to explore my identity, I found immense strength in my heritage. I delved into the stories of the struggles and triumphs my grandmother and mother had endured, discovering how they leaned on their faith in God to carry them through the most challenging times. Their resilience and unwavering belief became a source of inspiration for me, guiding me on my own journey of self-discovery and acceptance.

I surrounded myself with people who saw my true worth and celebrated my individuality rather than trying to diminish it. Those new relationships helped me rebuild my self-esteem and see myself through a lens of love and acceptance. Friends who uplifted me, mentors who guided me, and communities that embraced me all played crucial roles in my journey.

"Therefore, encourage one another and build each other up, just as in fact you are doing" (1 Thessalonians 5:11, NIV).

One of the most significant influences was my grandmother. Her wisdom and stories about our family's past instilled a deep sense of pride in me. She often said, *"Your skin is your armor, your lips are your voice, and your forehead holds the wisdom of generations."* Her words became a mantra, a source of strength during moments of doubt.

"Listen to your father, who gave you life, and do not despise your mother when she is old" (Proverbs 23:22, NIV).

By the time I reached my 30s, I had fully embraced my identity and no longer felt the need to conform to societal beauty standards. Instead, I celebrated my uniqueness and encouraged others to do the same. I became an advocate for self-love and acceptance, sharing my story to inspire others struggling with their self-image. I started speaking at schools and community centers, sharing my journey and the lessons I had learned. I wanted to reach out to young girls who, like me, felt out of place in their own skin. I wanted them to know that they were not alone and that their beauty was real and undeniable. Through those interactions, I found purpose and fulfillment, knowing that my experiences could help others find their own path to self-acceptance. Each talk, each conversation, was a step toward building a community where everyone felt valued and seen for who they truly were.

Looking back, I realized the journey was as important as the destination. Every challenge I faced, every moment of doubt, and every tear shed had shaped me into the strong, confident person I had become. My story was not just about overcoming adversity but about finding the strength to love myself unconditionally. Each step of the way, I learned more about who I was and what I was capable of. The pain in my past became the foundation of my strength.

I learned to forgive those who had hurt me, understanding that their actions reflected their insecurities, not my worth. That realization was liberating! It allowed me to release the burden of resentment and focus on my growth and happiness. The power of forgiveness was crucial in my journey. It wasn't about excusing the hurtful actions of others; it was about freeing myself from the grip of anger and bitterness. I came to understand that holding onto those negative emotions only hindered my progress. By letting go, I made space for healing and self-love. The process was not easy, but it was necessary for my transformation.

I also learned that vulnerability is not a weakness but a source of strength. By allowing myself to be vulnerable, I opened up to new experiences and deeper connections with others. I shared my story, my struggles, and my triumphs, and in doing so, I found a community of people who supported and uplifted me. That network of support was invaluable, providing me with the encouragement I needed to continue my journey.

One of the most profound lessons I learned was the power of self-love. Loving myself unconditionally meant accepting all parts of me — the good, the bad, and the imperfect. It meant recognizing my worth and treating myself with kindness and compassion. That shift in mindset was transformative, allowing me to see myself in a new light and embrace my true identity.

As I reflect on my journey, I realize that it is ongoing. There will always be new challenges to face and new lessons to learn, but I am no longer afraid. I have the tools and resilience to navigate whatever comes my way. My journey has taught me that I am capable of more than I ever imagined, and that true strength comes from within. Sharing my story has become a way to inspire others. I want people to know that they are not alone in their struggles and that overcoming adversity and finding self-acceptance is possible. By being open and honest about my journey, I hope to encourage others to embrace their own paths and find the strength to love themselves unconditionally.

Reflecting on my journey, I am filled with gratitude for the experiences that have shaped me. Every challenge, every moment of doubt, and every tear shed has contributed to my growth and transformation. I am proud of the person I have become, and I look forward to continuing my journey with confidence and self-love. My story is a testament to the power of resilience, forgiveness, and the unwavering belief in one's own worth.

QUIN LEVY

Dedication: My story is dedicated to my loving husband, who encouraged me to share a snippet from our love story. We've had phenomenal growth, and I'm delighted to be on this journey with you. Everything we endured was a process, yet I'm grateful God has kept us together by placing HIS love in our hearts.

Bio: Quin Levy is a devoted believer in Christ Jesus, a loving mother and wife, an author, and the CEO and Founder of the M. Ariel Love Foundation, a 501(c)(3) organization committed to domestic violence prevention. With a deep passion for writing poetry, Quin creatively captures real-life experiences in her work. Stay connected with her on Facebook and Instagram at Quin Levy, and learn more about her foundation by visiting http://www.mariellovefoundation.com. The M. Ariel Love Foundation is also active on Facebook, Instagram, and TikTok.

Tried and True

I remember it like it was yesterday. I was just coming off break at work, exiting the elevator, when my phone went "ding," indicating I had received a text message. I didn't recognize the number but read the text anyway:

"If you want to learn more about the fidelity of your husband, click the link."

It could have been spam, but I thought, *"What the heck,"* and clicked the link. When my husband's name flashed across the screen, my heart raced as I was laser-focused on the contents before me. Staring back at me was a secret email account I'd never seen before, with messages dating back months from and to the same female.

Before we get into the contents, let me give you a little background…

I am an attractive African American woman. I've never had a problem getting a man, much less getting them to take me seriously. I had two children out of wedlock, and although it isn't ideal, it taught me a lot about men and myself. I was less than two years into my first marriage and around 28 years old at the time of that text message. I'd passed on other marriage proposals, and although I wasn't always celibate, I wasn't into wasting my time on people I knew weren't it. I prayed that God would send me the husband He had just for me. You see, after my first heartbreak, my baby daddy's incarceration, and another boyfriend's untimely death, I knew I needed God to choose for me. So, to find out that this dude was cheating on me was simply mind-blowing!

God and I had a conversation. I mean, I was really trying to figure out if maybe I didn't hear Him correctly. Did I move in my flesh and decide to get married? I knew getting cheated on wasn't a part of the plan. I thought, *"God, you didn't allow the others. I need to know:* **WHAT IS THIS?!**" I couldn't even get through all the messages before calling him. I was fuming at the audacity! It has **ALWAYS** been my belief that "I am the prize." How dare he do this to me!

Tim was quiet, a great dad, hardworking, and caring. He was also nicely built, handsome, his mother's only son, and protective. What got me about him wasn't his looks or conversation but his attentiveness, work ethic, moral compass, and the fact that he was a good father. He was the kind of guy who went to work, cried if he couldn't see his son, and fixed things around the house without being asked. Not to mention, he knew how to fix cars and checked on his mom often. The only drawback was the "excitement" factor, but I went with it, hoping that it would develop with time. After dating for about a year and a half, we got married.

I ran downstairs to the lobby of my job to call him. 'Ring, Ring, Ring...' After the third ring, he answered. *"Hello?"* he said into the phone.

I was so angry that my hands were shaking uncontrollably. I immediately asked, *"Who is Dina?"* He acted like he had no idea who I was talking about. Yelling, I said, **"Yeah, your little secret is out! Your lil girlfriend has hired a private eye, and he contacted me, exposing everything!"** The phone fell silent. Without demanding a response, I ended the call, turned off my phone, and returned to work. For the remainder of that day, I struggled to focus on work.

Tim and I had just come off a separation about a month prior. Marriage had proven to be more challenging than either of us expected. We were both in our late twenties. Just one month after we were married, I found out I was pregnant. Tim's job was iffy, while I worked full-time to maintain the household. Although he tried, I **NEVER** signed up to take care of a man. I already had three kids; no way did I need a fourth. Tim complained that I spoke to him harshly, but it wasn't intentional. I honestly felt like he was not holding up his end of the bargain. Eventually, the fights started getting too intense, so he decided to make a run for it.

I was upset. I never wanted to get a divorce. I loved Tim and thought marriage was supposed to be forever. It literally felt like someone had died. He wouldn't take my calls or come home. He'd gone to his sister's house (from my knowledge), and he didn't have the type of family that would tell him what was right. Instead, they'd go along with whatever he did. I couldn't believe my marriage had taken such a turn.

Ever since I was a little kid, I knew I wanted to be a wife and have a family. Never had I pictured it like that. There I was, with an additional baby, egg-faced because I genuinely believed my marriage was forever. I felt hurt, let down, hopeless, and honestly, a little suicidal. Once I began having thoughts of self-harm, I knew it was nothing but the enemy. I knew suicide wasn't an option, but it's in those dark moments when the devil takes the opportunity to get into your ear and say things like, *"What's the point of life if you can't be happy?"* and *"They all just leave."* It was at that moment that I cried out to God. I prayed and leaned on Him. I dealt with my emotions and started to accept that this was where I was now, but it was not my end destination. Every day got a little better. I focused on the things I had, took care of my children, and eventually began to converse with other people just to occupy my mind. I missed Tim, but he'd shown me I was not who he wanted.

Three months passed, and though we'd met up for him to get his daughter, very few words were ever spoken between us. I'd come to terms with the fact that my marriage was over. The paperwork was the only formality left to tend to. Adultery is grounds for divorce, so God wasn't holding it against me. Still, it was not something I wanted. Growing up, my mother married multiple times. As a result, I always said I only wanted to be married once. However, I also realized that no matter how much you want to be with someone, you can't make them do right by you.

Kia's birthday was just around the corner, and I was planning a party. Obviously, with Tim being such a good father, he wanted to help and be involved in all the details. I welcomed his assistance, which opened the door to a casual conversation. He came over one Saturday morning to bring me some money for the party and asked me for a hug. As we embraced, I felt a sense of relief being released between our bodies. He whispered in my ear, *"I miss you."* God knows I missed him, too, but there were so many things we needed to talk about. As he returned to his car, he asked me out on a date. In my heart of hearts, I wanted our marriage to work, so I agreed. From that Saturday up until our date, we spoke daily. We'd both had time to think about what we'd done wrong, what we could do better, how we'd shown up for one another, and what we wanted.

Did we *really* want forever with one another? Ultimately, were we willing to put in the work and forsake all others?

There was no doubt that Tim's actions had broken my trust in him. There was a moment when I wanted to re-enact the scene from the movie *Waiting to Exhale* when Angela Bassett acted out in response to her hurt, but I was forced to look deeper. In no way was Tim's cheating okay, but I was of no help in the matter. I'd torn him down with my mouth and pushed him away with the callous way I behaved toward him. I can admit I was frustrated and immature. I took ownership of my part in the turmoil, and Tim took complete responsibility for his. Granted, no sin is greater than the other, but the consequences may differ. Tim understood that all ties were to be cut from that "Dina" character and that my trust was a work in progress.

Tim arrived to pick me up around 7:30 p.m. that following Saturday night. He approached the door with flowers. Once we got in the car, he looked at me, grabbed my hand, and said, *"You look beautiful. Can we start over?"*

I wanted to reply with a simple yes, but I needed to know he was serious. I had no desire to relive the circumstances that separated us in the first place. One thing I know is this: What you don't learn from, you'll likely repeat. I replied, *"Let's start slow."* He agreed.

That one date quickly spun into him being back home. I wish I could say that after that, life was peachy, but it was a long road to recovery. "Dina" was determined to share her pain and anger with me at the expense of my marriage, which I both did and did not understand because she knew he was married, but Tim allowed her both the space and ammunition to assault our relationship. It was a lot to swallow. I was in a marriage I wanted to be in with someone I thought I knew, but I found myself questioning everything. I never saw it coming, so I hadn't the slightest idea how to recover. I wanted to, though. ***Who was he? Was he the person I thought or the person I'd recently discovered?***

It wasn't long before I began questioning everything he said and everywhere he went. I was unstable in my marriage to the point of not wanting to plan trips or even change my last name. Not only was it hard for me, but it was difficult for him, too. He wanted me to trust him and just pick up as if nothing had happened, but that was impossible. He sometimes wanted to throw in the towel, fearing I'd never trust him again. Although I assured him I was trying, he was always free to leave if he wasn't willing to put in the work. He chose to stay and kept working on it. After years of rebuilding, prayer, and other life situations, we made our way back to solid ground, except this ground was tried and true.

I've learned that love is not always easy, but it's always worth it. Trust is easy to lose but hard to earn. God's love for the church is the perfect analogy to describe marriage.

Loving Tim through the pain and being committed to the marriage birthed some things in me. It showed me things I needed to change to love him properly. It realigned me with God's idea of what marriage should be and made it clear that marriage is His creation. We cannot do it without Him without loving the way He loves. It is impossible. Marriage is two imperfect people who change over time yet still choose to love one another despite differences, mistakes, views, and misunderstandings. We chose to love one another through the hurt, pain, highs, and lows. True love covers a multitude of sins. Matthew 19:6 (NIV) states, *"So they are no longer two, but one flesh. What therefore God has joined together, let no man separate."* Our marriage is a living, thriving witness that if you do it God's way and give it to Him, He can fix it. Have faith in His Word, as He is surely watching over His Word to perform it.

FAITH MAKOWA

Dedication: I dedicate this chapter to the Body of Christ in order to bring consolation, strength, and inspiration. May you be reminded that difficulty is not the end but rather a chance for development and refinement. Remain steadfast, regardless of the cost.

Bio: Faith Makowa is a multifaceted individual with diverse skills and experiences, all dedicated to making a difference. She has authored books and articles on personal development, leadership, spirituality, and family. As a Speaker and Servant of God, she shares her knowledge through workshops and online conferences, empowering people, families, and communities.

Cradled in Unwavering Promises

The day was filled with anticipation and excitement, but it swiftly turned into agony as disaster struck, interrupting my routine. What started as a typical shopping trip with my children ended in excruciating pain and fear when a reminder of the unpredictability of life and the consequence of remaining purpose in the face of adversity reared its ugly head.

In preparation for attending a prophetic conference — an event I had eagerly awaited for months — we were picking out new clothes and planned on indulging in a treat afterward. As time ticked by, I envisioned the host of promising speakers, a stirring worship experience, and a community of believers. My heart was light, filled with expectation for the blessings that awaited me. Little did I realize that the day would forever shape my concept of faith and God's faithfulness.

After browsing our local supermarket's shelves, we approached the checkout. I reached into my handbag to retrieve my wallet, only to be greeted by a wave of terror. My heart sank. Fear flooded my mind. My bag was wide open, and my wallet was missing! In that heart-stopping moment, reality hit hard: my cards, cash, and ID had disappeared without a trace. My inquiry to the cashier, asking them to check the store's security footage, only added to the sinking feeling in my stomach when I learned there were no cameras inside the store.

It felt like the world had come crashing down on me. Fear and disbelief coursed through my feelings. I felt violated by the circumstances, confronted by the tumultuous nature of life: Darkness tried its best to defeat me. It was not just a loss of a wallet but an invasion of my peace and sense of safety. I felt lost and vulnerable. My tears left a trail on my blouse as I questioned, *"Why would God allow this to be, especially on a day meant for spiritual growth?"* The excitement about the conference fizzled into a dull ache. Time seemed to freeze. Suddenly, thoughts of the inconveniences of replacing my ID and canceling my cards weighed heavily on my mind. I immediately asked the shop manager to allow me to make several calls, managing to communicate with each bank that my wallet was stolen. With a heavy heart and weary spirit, I left the store to file a police report—a necessary step yet enormously disheartening given recent events. The officer on duty was compassionate, but I was filled with doubt about recovery. At that moment, I became a shadow of my former self.

Amid the chaos and doubt, something within me stirred the profound faithfulness of God manifesting, illuminating the shadows that had momentarily eclipsed my soul. A still, reassuring voice prompted me to seek solace at the church where I had registered for a prophetic ministry. Taking a deep breath, I made the decision to go. My children, seeing my torture but still filled with childhood strength, accompanied me without question. When we arrived, my pastor received us with open arms and an understanding hint in her eyes. She invited us to sit and took time to listen as I recited the details of my day. I was immediately assured by her compassion and support.

As we all know, our community is an important force, and that day, it worked miraculously. My pastor provided emotional support and revived us with words of encouragement and hope—a simple yet profound act of kindness that reminded me of the strength of human connection. In those moments of sharing, my worries slowly dissipated. We laughed and ate, and I realized then that life would go on, not just in moments of triumph but also in the face of adversity. The angel of my circumstances (as I like to call my experience) served as a reminder that even in our darkest moments, quiet strength can guide us to places of comfort and hope.

Still feeling overwhelmed, I made my way to the conference venue from the church dining hall. My heart was heavy, but I was determined. As I entered the sanctuary, the atmosphere was electric with the presence of God. Worship commenced, and it was as if the heaviness of the day began to lift. I surrendered my burden to Him, allowing His Spirit to wash over me. Amid the praise and worship, I first saw the faithfulness of God manifesting in my life. The church prayed for peace for my family, and the pastor told the church that they knew what to do when someone had been robbed. It would be an understatement to say that their support was incredible!

The act of reaching out to my spiritual community converted a day marred by loss into one filled with a renewed sense of faith, connection, and gratefulness. I was blown away by the sacrificial love abounding in that community. It illuminated the darkness of my recent experience.

During the conference, the messages shared resonated deeply within me. The speaker was a well-known seer. He stepped up to me, beaming brightly, and began the tale of my life. *"Woman of faith,"* he began, *"you always teach people to reclaim what belongs to them, whether it is physical or an intangible essence of self-worth. Why didn't you do the same?"* Before I could respond, he said, *"There's a particular ache that comes when someone else takes credit for your hard work. History repeats itself. Seven years ago, your white handbag was stolen, and today, your wallet was stolen again, containing items that you consider your identity?"* That just blew my mind! I felt like I had been stabbed in the heart. Anguish transformed into bitterness, reminding me how my identity always slipped through my grasp.

I clearly remember when someone stole my handbag through the window. My ID was in the inside pocket. Weeks turned into months. Then, one day, a friend of mine found my ID slightly crumpled but intact. About my hard work: That was something that seemingly happened with every connection. My ideas, time, and efforts were often stolen as well. I would watch as others stood and basked in the limelight while my contributions faded into the background. I felt insignificant at those times, sensing that my sweat and tears were in vain. I felt like a shadow each time as I watched someone else claim accolades that rightfully belonged to me.

So, I lived in those threads of loss and robbery of my identity woven into my journey with resentment that simmered into fierce anger. I sometimes asked God, *"Why am I experiencing such things in my life? Can't You protect me from such robbery?"* But He had a way of turning my pain into purpose. My faith and resilience helped me stitch together the frayed edges of my remaining self-worth. Although it took me years to learn important lessons about those experiences, through reaffirmation and perseverance, when events like those happened, I never allowed envy or bitterness to mold. Instead, I leaned into God's promise that our labor is not in vain.

Life may sweep us off our feet at times, but we have the power to stand tall. We are anchored by faith.

During the conference, another speaker emphasized the importance of communication and listening to the dreams God gives us. A few months before the robbery, I had a vivid dream-turned-nightmare where I realized my brand-new car was stolen and burned to ashes, but I ignored it as "just anxiety." I came to understand that God had tried to warn me, but I neglected to pay attention to His warning.

Each trial I faced had a purpose. They not only taught me the strength of my calling but also to remain steadfast, knowing that even on a shadowy path, there is light. My identity, security, and sense of self-worth in the physical may be robbed, but God's glory will always emerge, revealing the power of faith in a miraculous God. I was confronted with the fact that my true value does not come from material goods or public recognition. It is embedded in my relationship, faithfulness to His calling, and the way in which He gives unexpected grace.

That day marked a turning point in my life. I learned to find security in God's Word and appreciate His unwavering faithfulness. I think about the story of the Apostle "Doubting" Thomas in the Bible and how he experienced moments of doubt. Like him, I am reminded of God's ever-present grace. I have also learned that loyalty is a two-way road. Just as I commit to serving Him, He remains devoted to guiding and providing for me.

Sometimes, life seems unfair, especially when we face insurmountable and unanticipated challenges, but God remains faithful.

After the conference, as we prepared to return home, and just when God allowed my disappointments to crown my day, someone called to tell me that my wallet had been found!

A fleeting thought passed through my mind: *"Can the thief take my identity?"* I quieted that voice by responding, ***"No! What is genuinely true can never be stolen!"***

Upon arriving home, I observed a Sister-in-Christ pacing in front, holding my wallet in her hand. When she handed it to me, I quickly rifled through it, noticing its poorly damaged state. Everything was there except the cash. Since godly hands orchestrated everything, I was not just reunited with my identity cards but also my identity. Tears streamed down my face as I considered God's endless faithfulness at the positive turn of events. It felt like I had received a double portion of God's blessings! It reflected His restorative power each time something was taken from me. I'm grateful for the community of believers who rallied around me, proving that the Body of Christ is a living testament of God's love.

That cataclysmal day turned into a testament of faithfulness and transformation. I emerged from what formerly felt like a woeful moment, converted and empowered by the implausible experiences of trust in God's faithfulness. I learned to be more attuned to the warnings God sends, whether through dreams or a still, small voice within.

As I reflect on that day, I treasure the memory of God's provision during that unexpected trial. I discovered that amid chaos, there is beauty in faith, love in community, and power in listening to God's whispers. I entered that prophetic conference expecting exposures, but a profound lesson was learned: God is faithful and always working for our good, even when we do not see it in the natural.

I encourage you to persevere in your faithfulness and push forward in your calling. Indeed, the *"thief comes to steal, kill, and destroy"* (John 10:10) when others take credit for your works. Be empowered, knowing others have faced similar trials and tribulations and come out stronger than before. Yes, it's difficult to embrace the pain during each challenge you face, but seek out the lesson and allow God to transform your struggles into steppingstones rather than obstacles. While life may sometimes leave us feeling "robbed," learn to understand that loss often leads to lessons, growth, and a deeper understanding of God's unwavering presence.

    I have come to understand the significance of being a faithful servant. It is not simply about enduring difficulties; it is about trusting in God's goodness despite our circumstances. As I think about the times my identity was stolen, I remain thankful for the path I have walked and the faithfulness of God. I recognized the beauty in my struggles and learned that every brokenness may lead us to a different expression of our purpose, which aligns further with God's plan for our lives. No theft—whether material or recognition—can ever diminish His faithfulness for us.

ALLAINA MARIA

Dedication: To my big sister, Yolonda Williams, who was a victim of domestic violence, your life and legacy will never be in vain. I'll tell your story far and wide. Long live Yolonda Williams & Darryl J. Ford, Sr.

Bio: Allaina Maria is the CEO of Allaina Maria 360 LLC, Actress, Singer/Songwriter, Multi-genre Author, Screenwriter, International Motivational Speaker, and Entrepreneur. Her mission is to cultivate motivation and self-reflection through high-quality, comprehensive discussions and entertainment that stimulates personal growth, challenges perspectives, and entertains and uplifts spirits. She desires to provide quality 360 services through motivational speaking, music, films, and books. Allaina Maria is the youngest of three girls and a Daytona Beach, Florida native. She is the mother of two beautiful daughters who fuel her everyday life. Her life's mantra is to give life everything she's got because the world is her playground!

Judas Was Me

December 2022 is a month I will never forget. I recall my sister Shawna calling me and yelling into the phone with evident distress. My panicked cries of **"What happened?"** matched the angst in her voice. *"Uncle Darryl is gone,"* she declared.

My mind turned upside down. I couldn't seem to process the words, even as the hairs on the back of my neck rose and my natural body prepared itself to respond. In utter shock, I replied, *"Ex-squeeze me?"* I had never used that word before. As a matter of fact, I don't think that word is in the dictionary, yet that word was an appropriate reply for such a fake declaration of death. Well, at least that is what I hoped was the case. Unfortunately, it was not. Indeed, he was gone. The cold, hard reality of that gut-wrenching truth hit me like a ton of bricks. The shockwaves of grief, confusion, and hurt rang out in my head like firecrackers on the 4th of July.

Although we all know that death is a part of life, that knowledge does not lessen the trauma to one's emotions that is associated with death.

My pain trumped all sense and sensibility. To me, my uncle was too young to die. He was too loved to leave this world when he did. *"Why so soon?"* I asked God. I didn't understand why my uncle's death was chosen so suddenly… so unexpectedly. Looking back now, whether I had a warning or not, his death would have broken my family and me, no matter how you sliced it. His presence meant so much to all of us, and his absence created a gaping maw in our hearts.

The days leading up to his funeral were horrible, to say the least. The anticipation of seeing his body lie in state assaulted my emotions recklessly. My grandmother, Jeanette Thomas, birthed two girls and six boys. Uncle Darryl was number five of eight. Their chain was irretrievably broken. The grief of his loss was a heavy load and a catapult at the same time. My uncle left such an amazing legacy on and within this earth. Much like we all do, he had plans for "tomorrow" that were never realized, as the grave robbed him of a new breath.

Uncle Darryl's death ignited a fire within me. His exit from this life pushed me to see me. His death helped me to see how giving the grave any of my potential didn't make sense. God gave me gifts, talents, and abilities, yet I sat on them. The cares of life had taught me to play life in the safety zone and not to ruffle feathers. I chose to "just exist." My uncle's absence, however, pushed me to live! I forced myself to dig deep and become the best version of Allaina Maria.

In January 2023, I sat on my couch, and the story of *Mariah* (my first Urban Fiction novel) came into my head. I had never written a book before but found the inspiration to put my pen to paper and create. I wrote that novel and began preparation to release the book, and then "Fear" showed up. Fear didn't grant me the courtesy of knocking on the door; it had a key and let itself in. Fear also brought along its best friend, "Imposter Syndrome," and that voice was boisterous!

"No one wants to read your books!"
"You are not a real author!"
"You are just doing something to be doing something!"
"You will not make one sale!"
"No one wants that mess!"

Those were just a few of the words that plagued me—to the point that I almost withdrew from releasing my project. The words of self-doubt fought me hard. I would look in the mirror and see the fear of doing something new staring back at me until I had an epiphany: I realized that I had become my own Judas. The Allaina Maria of today was sabotaging the growth of the Allaina Maria to come. I discovered my thoughts were my own. No one told me not to write or that I was no good; it was the Judas within me! As long as I believed those words, they were my truth. Stinking thinking and my warped perception of my gift of writing were my reality. My humanity was so strong and filled with doubt that I didn't give reverence to God's divinity.

I grew up in the church all my life, and I didn't recall stinking thinking being written anywhere in the scriptures. One passage that replayed in my head repeatedly was, *"For the gifts and callings of God are without repentance"* (Romans 11:29). What that scripture means to me is that if you are alive, you, too, can have a gift. There is no respect of person regarding gifts.

I embraced that it was okay to have and use my gift. I belonged as a writer. I was free to write and should do so with the utmost confidence. I trusted God and His infinite wisdom to go forth, but I had to first silence the noise in my mind and meditate on His Word. As a result, in June 2023, I released *Mariah*—and did so successfully! Since then, I have released a ten-part *Healing From* journal series, a two-part children's book series titled *Cir the Circle*, and have co-authored five anthologies. In addition, I write monthly for two separate magazines as a contributing writer.

But it doesn't stop there!

The ability to silence the noise and hear God's voice has catapulted me to unlock other sides of Allaina Maria. I began my motivational speaking journey and have been afforded opportunities to speak both stateside and internationally. I have since launched my company and am CEO Allaina Maria 360. I am also a singer/songwriter, actress, and screenwriter. Those things are not mentioned to boast of my goodness but rather to tell of the goodness of God and my faith in Him and His Word.

Just imagine what my life would be like if I hadn't trusted the God in me to become a better version of me. I would still be a shadow of myself, allowing fear to direct my path. I would not have accomplished or completed everything I have been blessed to do.

To the reader: I want to make an appeal to you today. I encourage you to hold on and trust God. I want you to cultivate and manifest those goals and dreams you have had since childhood. Some dreams you have shared, and some you wouldn't dare utter because, like the older version of me, you fear the unknown. I implore you to take the next step and watch God be right there with you every step of the way.

Don't be your own Judas by betraying the higher version of yourself in your current state. Silence the noise! Open your mouth and decree and declare freedom over every part of your being!

Following is an ode to the death of Judas:

Judas Was Necessary

Judas was necessary to show you, you,
To illuminate the light on the things that you do.
Judas was necessary to open your eyes,
To show you yourself and remove the disguise.
Judas was necessary to shake up some things,
To help unravel the fear that clings.
Judas was necessary to disrupt the old,
To plant new seeds of hope for your soul.
Judas was necessary to remind you of the past,
To warn you that the old season couldn't last.
Judas was necessary to reveal your strength,
To let you know you can go any length.
Judas was necessary because he had to die,
To let you live, walk, run, then fly.
Judas is now dead, and you are healing,
Now walking in your purpose, your life is fulfilling.
Your faith is unmovable; your resolve is sure.
Your assignment is clear, and your heart is pure.
The experience with Judas taught you how to fight;
It showed you your strength and your might.
Look at you now, walking in destiny,
Owning everything that God said you can be.
The world looks on, seeing your glory,
But now is the time to tell your stories.
Use your voice to help your fellow man,
As they are dealing with their Judas, and you know firsthand
The struggle of accepting that Judas was you;

Share tips and tools on how you got through.
But please don't forget to share God's love;
His grace is sufficient and as gentle as a dove.
Remind them of His faithful heart
That has never wavered from the start.
Don't stop striving; don't lose your pep.
Continue to ask God to order your steps.
Never get haughty or too puffed up;
Be confidently bold, but let the Lord fill your cup.

As you read this chapter, I pray that you find hope. I pray my words are strength to your navel and marrow to your very bones, providing fortitude during those times when your faith may want to waver. Always remember God's faithfulness toward us and His great sacrifice He made on Calvary's cross.

Judas **WAS** me — past tense — but not anymore.

Judas **WAS** you, but he had to die so that you and I may live freely and abundantly!

MIN. JIMMY MERCHANT

Dedication: This chapter honors those who, like Job, remain unshakable in their faith amid life's challenges. May your steadfast belief inspire others to push through, knowing that even in the darkest times, their faith provides enduring power when they wholly trust God the Father.

Bio: Jimmy Merchant is best known for his contributions to music as an original founding member of the Doo-Wop vocal group Frankie Lymon and The Teenagers. To his credit, he is a co-writer of their greatest hit song, *Why Do Fools Fall in Love*. He has performed globally and in PBS music specials, television commercials, and on-screen movies. In 1993, he and his group were inducted into the Rock and Roll Hall of Fame. Jimmy is a minister of the Gospel, often preaching End-Time messages. He and his beautiful wife, Mary, reside in the Bronx, New York.

Job: The Faith-filled Man of God

In the Holy Bible, the Old Testament Book of Job tells the story of a blameless, upright man named Job who feared God and shunned evil. Although his story is not entirely written by him, it remains an incredible and powerful spiritual account of **FAITH**. Importantly, it was placed in the Bible as a very needed story of God written primarily for men. The gist of Job's story is this: Despite being blessed with comfort and riches, he was suddenly hit hugely by a series of attacks on his life. He lost everything and wrestled with the question, *"Why?!"* When all was said and done, God blessed Job again and even added 140 more years to his life, along with four generations of children. It must be noted that all throughout his suffering from great losses, he maintained his integrity.

Reflecting on the lesson from Job's story, men are encouraged to stay real and true to God, even while going through great trials and tribulations in life (even moreso in this world's crazy last days).

Job's name is referenced as 'Jashub' in the first Book of the Bible (Genesis 46:10). The name 'Job' is mentioned in 1 Chronicles 7:1 as one of the sons of Issachar. While the 42 chapters of the Book of Job show the generic word for God to be Elohim, its clear truth is that there is only **ONE GOD**. Without going into its theatrical layout here, the Book of Job is an accurate account of what happened in that man's life for us all to observe and perhaps understand our inability to come to grips with God's personal care for us.

Think about it like this: God knows everything—the good, the bad, and the ugly about us—yet He still steps in to protect and save His children, even as we try to determine why bad things happen to good people. Nonetheless, God has all the answers, so our faith in Him must be tried and true… **first and foremost.**

Job was a Godly man who trusted and believed in His Creator wholeheartedly, yet he had no way of knowing why he experienced terrible tragedies in his life. *Why did God allow Satan to take everything away from him?* Scripture tells us that Satan believed Job honored God solely because of the way God blessed him. As we learn, **Satan was mistaken**!

Notably, as Job grieved deeply, he never cursed God. That demonstrates to us that Satan cannot bring destruction into our lives when God's power lives within us. That, my friend, is where our consistent faith should be. In fact, James (one of the last four writers of the Bible) importantly states that Job's perseverance through over-the-top suffering is an example of how we are to carry and maintain ourselves with the aid of God, who is full of compassion and mercy (read James 5:10-11).

Job 1:21-22 represents Job on God's behalf, instructing us to maintain our faith in God, even as we are being tested. As believers, the Book of Job should be relevant reading, as it aids us in knowing we should not feel that personal troubles are "unfair." Although we may often not fully comprehend why we suffer and may even blame ourselves, understand that suffering is used at times to purify, test, teach, and strengthen our hearts toward God, knowing that He is in complete control of all things and circumstances in our lives. Yes, Job lost his family and wealth, but he did not lose his health or God's blessings.

Job is the 18th book in the Bible's Old Testament (between Esther and Psalms), written by someone unknown. Yet I find it important to note that God refers to Job as "My servant" four times. Those two words show God's approval as Job discusses his painful experience with friends. In fact, 34 of the 42 chapters make us realize that God is, indeed, in full control.

I came to grips with that when I became a man of God in 1985 after great musical fame and a harrowing bout of street life (I penned the first half of my autobiography in a book titled *A Teenager's Dream*, published by our dear, darling Angela Edwards, who is much like a loving daughter to me). Even as we're working on the second half, which includes when I became a minister for God to the present age of 84, I pray that this writing serves its intentional purpose in the Name of Jesus. Amen.

As mentioned previously, Job 1:1 states that he was blameless and upright. In summary, after unknowingly being attacked by Satan (permitted by God), he immediately says, *"Naked I came from my mother's womb, and naked I will depart. The LORD gave, and the LORD has taken away; may the name of the LORD be praised"* (Job 1:21). Before diving into his story and all that he endured, we are shown Job's Godly faith. When the LORD spoke to Job, He asked, *"Who is this that darkens MY COUNSEL with words without knowledge?"* (Job 38:1-2). Job then makes plainly clear this wisdom: *"My ears had heard of You but now my eyes have seen You. Therefore, I despise myself and repent in dust and ashes"* (Job 42:5-6).

Overall, our responsibility to God is to **obey** Him, **trust** Him, and **submit** to His will, whether we understand it or not (read Isaiah 55:8-9).

****

Before I go…

Being a family man with children, grands, and great-grands and reflecting on the end of Job's story concerning him having ten children (read Job 42:14), I was led to briefly make a necessary notation regarding a unique woman in the Bible. After Job's seven sons are mentioned, his three daughters are referenced by name. The meaning of each name is sidelined in my King James Study Bible, which I believe shows us the importance of women in the Scriptures. Those names are:

- ❖ **Jemimah** (Handsome as the Day)
- ❖ **Cassia** (A fragrance)
- ❖ **Keren-happuch** (The Horn of Color)

Wow! I actually saw the spiritual importance of those three women elsewhere, as they stand out biblically in terms of their beauty.

After talking with God and reviewing various female Bible scenarios, I was led to the following phenomenal, unusual story found in Luke 7:36-50. Simon (a Pharisee) had invited Jesus and others to his home to sit and eat with him, but he did not show Jesus simple gestures of common hospitality while greeting Him. Then, during the meal, while others were appalled to see a sinful woman in Simon's house among those so-called respected men, Jesus made it clear to them that she, in fact, outdid them all when she showed Jesus incredible love from her heart as she washed His feet with her tears and dried them with her hair while being very sorrowful for her sins. Right then and there, Jesus forgave her and told her she was free from all the distress she experienced because of her sins.

God had an amazing love for His servant Job and the female sinner in the aforementioned story. Incredibly, He continues to work behind the scenes in the present day. At the time of this writing, He has placed a 'Black female' Vice President in a position to possibly become the President of the United States, going against all untruth followers in these unequaled critical times. God alone is the Master Creator of all things in the universe. He desires that we lovingly succeed faithfully on His behalf and not go along with lying leaders. Sadly, being in love with God seems foolish to many people. That couldn't be further from the truth.

As an 'End-Time Minister' called by God and led by the Holy Spirit to constantly be in touch with Him (as all true believers should be), I believe it's imperative to know and live by God's **truth**. Whether male or female, as you walk your faith walk, consider Job's story, that of the sinful woman who washed Jesus' feet with her tears, and the moment Jesus lovingly wiped His disciples' feet, displaying His humility (read John 3:1-17).

"For by grace, you have been saved through faith. And this is not your own doing; it is the gift of God, not a result of works, so that no one may boast" (Ephesians 2:8-9).

Many thanks, my dear friends. May God bless you all!

Minister James "Jimmy" Merchant

KATINA RICE-DAVIS

Dedication: To my late husband Eric, whose memory I hold dear. Your love and strength inspired me to keep moving forward. This chapter is dedicated to you, my guiding light. May your legacy shine through these words and bring hope to those on their own journey of grief and faith.

Bio: Katina Rice-Davis is a native of Cross Anchor, South Carolina. She studied at Winthrop University and USC – Upstate University. She is a two-time Bestselling Author and Speaker. Katina is also a staff writer for The Woodruff Times. She is the widow of Eric Davis and the mother of two. Additionally, she has one grandson, Sa'Mauri. Katina's hobbies include reading, writing, journaling, and watching true crime. Her mission is to inspire and motivate young women traveling the path of losing a spouse or significant other, leaving them to raise children alone. To contact Katina, email her at ykdavis43@gmail.com.

Anchored in Faith: A Journey Through Grief and Healing

The day my husband Eric passed away unexpectedly, my world shattered into a million pieces. The silence was deafening, the emptiness suffocating. I felt like I was drowning in a sea of despair, unable to find a lifeline to cling to. But then, I remembered the words of my late grandmother: *"Faith is the anchor that holds us steady in the midst of life's storms."* My grandmother was strong in her faith, and her words became my mantra through my grief journey.

I thought back to the day we met and the vows we shared on a sunny summer day. Our life together was a beautiful tapestry woven with love, laughter, and adventure. Now, a part of me was gone, and I felt lost and alone, left to raise our two young toddlers. The weight of my husband's passing settled upon me like a shroud. The ache within me felt like a chasm, impossible to bridge. I began to battle with anxiety and depression for quite some time.

The Bible addresses anxiety in various passages, offering guidance and encouragement. As I journaled, I often referred to a few verses that helped comfort me during my battle. Here are some key verses I often read:

- **Philippians 4:6-7 (NIV):** *"Do not be anxious about anything, but in every situation, by prayer and petition, with thanksgiving, present your requests to God. And the peace of God, which transcends all understanding, will guide your hearts and your minds in Christ Jesus."*

- **Matthew 6:25-34 (NIV):** In this passage, Jesus teaches us not to worry about life's necessities, as God provides for His children.
- **1 Peter 5:7 (NIV):** *"Cast all your anxiety on Him because He cares for you."*
- **Psalm 55:22 (NIV):** *"Cast your cares on the Lord, and He will sustain you."*
- **Proverbs 3:5-6 (NIV):** *"Trust in the Lord with all your heart and lean not on your own understanding; in all your ways, submit to Him, and He will make your paths straight."*
- **Isaiah 41:10 (NIV):** *"So, do not fear, for I am with you; do not be frightened, for I am your God. I will strengthen you and help you; I will uphold you with My righteous right hand."*

Those verses encourage us to:
➢ Pray and present our concerns to God.
➢ Trust in God's provision and care.
➢ Cast our anxieties on Him.
➢ Lean on His understanding, not our own.
➢ Fear not, for God is with us.

The Bible acknowledges anxiety but encourages us to bring it to God, trusting in His peace, provision, and guidance. During my grief journey and even now, those verses are impactful on my faith as well.

In the days that followed my husband's death, I wandered through the darkness, searching for answers. **Why had he been taken from me? Why must I endure this pain?** God whispered promises in the dead of night, *"You are not alone."* The gentle breeze that soothes my soul, *"I am with you, always."* The comforting embrace that wrapped around my shattered heart, *"You are loved."* And in that moment, I knew I would emerge from the darkness, scarred but stronger, my faith a beacon illuminating the path ahead. But with my faith being tested, I had to take it one day at a time.

Months later, I found solace in the Book of Psalms. One day, while reading scripture, I came across Psalm 34:18 (NIV): *"The Lord is close to the brokenhearted and saves the crushed in spirit."* Tears streamed down my face as I felt God's presence wrap around me like a warm blanket. I realized that my faith wasn't about avoiding pain or hardship but finding hope in the midst of it.

As I continued my grief journey, I encountered others who had walked similar paths. Their stories reminded me that I wasn't alone in my grief and that others had walked the path and found hope in their faith. It reminded me that my faith wasn't a solo journey but a communal one. Along the way, we could support and uplift each other during sorrow. Surrounding myself with people with strong faith had a profound, positive impact on my life. Being around those people provided encouragement and support during my difficult time. They also deepened my understanding of my faith and spiritual growth. They offered valuable wisdom and guidance when I needed it. Surrounding yourself with people who have strong faith is not about comparing or competing but about supporting and uplifting one another in your spiritual journeys.

The months passed, yet the ache of my husband's absence remained. It became a familiar companion, a reminder of the love we shared. My faith became the bridge that connected me to him and the promise that we would meet again in eternity. It helped me cherish the time we had rather than lament what could never be again.

Raising our two young children alone seemed like an insurmountable task. One day, while reading the Word, I came across Matthew 17:20 (NIV): *"If you have faith as small as a mustard seed, you can say to this mountain, 'Move from here to there,' and it will move."* I felt a glimmer of hope. I realized that it only took a little bit of faith, that our "mountain"/"grief journey" would move, and that the journey was only temporary. Then, I recalled one of my favorite passages, Matthew 21:22 (ESV): *"And whatever you ask in prayer, you will receive if you have faith."* I prayed fervently, asking God to give me the strength and wisdom to raise our children. As I navigated the challenges of single parenthood, my faith was my anchor. I held onto God's promises, reminding myself that He was my rock, my provider, and my comforter. I knew He had never left nor forsaken me all my life, so I continued to trust in Him.

My children became my motivation. I wanted them to see God's love and faithfulness in my life. I started sharing Bible stories with them, praying with them, and showing them God's love in action. With time, I saw the seeds of faith sprouting in their lives, as they were very active in our church. I knew God was still with us, guiding us through the storm. Raising young children after the loss of my spouse was a daunting task, but with faith, it became manageable. My faith held me steady. My faith was the rock that gave me strength and the comforter that wiped away my many tears. As a family, we learned to trust God's plan, even when we didn't understand it, and amid uncertainty, in time, we found peace.

My faith during my grief was crucial. It provided comfort and solace, helping to ease the pain and emotional distress. It gave me hope and strength to navigate the darkness and uncertainty while offering a broader perspective, reminding me that my situation was not the end. Faith facilitated my emotional healing by promoting acceptance of my loss. With my faith, I became resilient, which enabled me to cope with adversity. Having faith reminded me of the eternal perspective: ***Our loved ones are not gone forever.***

In the end, faith didn't erase my grief; it transformed it. It reminded me that I am not alone and that God is with me, always. It showed me that even in the darkest moments, there is hope—a hope that whispers, "You are loved, you are strong, and you will rise again." I chose to remain faithful as He guided my steps. I understood that it was only a season and that God was strengthening me to walk confidently through my situation. My new confidence has allowed me to share my testimony with others through speaking and writing. God is doing so much in my life right now as I better understand the plan He has been laying for me. I was a little fearful at first, but I understood that I had to move by faith to progress in my life. So, through all the pain and hurt I experienced, God has provided "greater."

When we take a leap of faith, our path may not always be clear. We must hold onto the conviction that God is leading us. Just as an anchor is securely fixed yet allows for movement and flexibility, faith gives us the freedom to navigate life's journey with confidence, adaptability, and resilience.

Faith and grief are not mutually exclusive; they are intertwined. My faith in God held me steady during my life's storm. I had to walk by faith and not by sight, meaning that my life was guided by faith, not by what I saw or understood. The whispered promise, the gentle breeze, and the comforting embrace wrapped around my shattered heart. It reminded me that I am not alone and that God is with me, always. And in that knowledge, I found hope—a hope that guided me on my journey of healing and restoration.

May our faith be the anchor that holds us steady… a constant reminder of God's **love, presence,** and **guidance** in our lives.

GENAE KULAH

Dedication: This is dedicated to my Sorors from Zeta Phi Beta Sorority, Incorporated, and my church family at Brister Baptist Church. When I went to that dark place, you would not allow me to move in but kept lighting the path so I could step out of darkness into God's marvelous light.

Bio: Coach/Pastor Genae Kulah is the Founder of The Fabric of Her Mind Coaching Group and The Word 4 H.E.R. Ministry. She is also the Executive Pastor and Prophetic Voice for the Preachers in Sneakers ministry powered by the Pink Pulpit International Convention of Women. She has a master's in biblical studies and certification as a Mental Health Coach specializing in Crisis Response and Trauma and Suicide Prevention, Biblical Counseling, Critical Incident Chaplain, and Domestic Violence and Human Trafficking Caseworker and Advocate. Genae is a bestselling author and a proud member of Zeta Phi Beta Sorority, Incorporated.

Walking in Faith With the Pain of Reality

"Immediately, the father of the child cried out and said with tears, 'Lord, I believe; help my unbelief!'" (Mark 9:24, NKJV)

That verse has always been special to me because it shows man's duality. It is easy for us to believe and walk in faith for the little things, but what do you do when faith says, *"You are healed,"* when, in reality, you are not? Every morning, you praise God for a new day. Your spirit is uplifted, but your mind, body, and soul want to stay in bed with the covers pulled up to your neck and the curtains closed because you know that once you set your feet on the ground, your reality will hit you. The things you used to be able to do, you are no longer able-bodied. A cloud of depression threatens to take you under. Sometimes, it would be so easy to allow it. All the while, your spirit says, *"Fight the good fight of faith. God is with you."*

And so, the day begins.

Typically, when I write a faith story concerning my life, I have difficulty deciding which one because God has been so good to me throughout my life. He has healed me from various trials such as abuse, trauma, and my "Prodigal Daughter" escapades. I will praise and give Him glory always. Oh, the joy of being delivered and set free! I'm grateful the blood of Jesus covers my past!

This time, however, I am writing while going through trials and tribulations. I am walking in faith with the pain of reality.

****

In 2023, I began my wellness journey. I wanted to be whole in my mind, body, and spirit because those three aspects of my life needed to align with the Word of God. I felt that people should be able to see me and see God in me, working through me, so I had to get myself together. My body, which is the temple of the Holy Spirit, did not look cared for. I was challenged by the words found in Romans 12:1 (NKJV), which says, *"I appeal to you therefore, brothers, by the mercies of God, to present your bodies as a living sacrifice, holy and acceptable to God, which is your spiritual worship."* I began taking classes at the gym, eating right, making weekly spa visits, and studying to become a Wellness Coach and a Zumba instructor. I am pleased to say I accomplished those goals.

I then started weight training. That was extremely challenging, but my **"I will not be defeated"** mindset kicked in, and I became stronger and toned. *I can wave my arm, and the flab won't keep going when I stop!* I know some of you ladies can relate. (Smile!) I also started losing weight and sharing what I learned with my spiritual and sorority sisters.

Now, on to my mind. Well, what can I say other than it really needed to be renewed? My mindset challenge came from Romans 12:2 (ESV), which says, *"Be not conformed to this world, but be transformed by the renewal of your mind, that by testing you may discern what is the will of God, what is good and acceptable and perfect."* I had to adopt a mindset that looked more like Christ and less like the effects of trauma and abuse. Many times, what we think is normal mental processing is actually a faulty mindset based on limited beliefs or cognitive distortions. *"Cognitive distortions are biased thoughts that can distort the way people see themselves, their lives, their specific day-to-day situations, their relationships, and other people. Those thoughts can contribute to mental health conditions such as depression and anxiety."* (medicalnewstoday.com)

Here are a few examples of cognitive distortions:

- **All-or-Nothing/Polarized Thinking:** This distortion is also known as "Black-and-White Thinking," and it occurs when a person is not able to see the gray areas of any situation.
- **Overgeneralization:** In this distortion, a person overgeneralizes things in their life, such as defining a single occurrence as an overall pattern.
- **Jumping to Conclusions** (making assumptions or mind-reading): This distortion happens when we assume what the other person is thinking or their intentions.
- **Magnification (Catastrophizing) or Minimization:** This distortion is when you exaggerate the meaning of something or, on the other extreme, minimize it.
- **Personalization:** This distortion involves us taking things personally and blaming ourselves for something in an illogical way.

After learning about the mind, I realized that I needed God and therapy. God healed me and brought me out, but the aftereffects remained. I was extremely excited because I was doing things that contributed to my wholeness in Christ and seeing results! So, you can imagine how I felt when, within three months, I went from exercising, dancing, and serving in the community to being unable to place my feet on the ground without pain.

In November 2023, I started feeling pain going down my leg every time I tried to walk. I thought it was sciatica pain, so the doctor prescribed medication. Unfortunately, the pain did not stop. The doctor thought it was arthritis, but the test results revealed that it was not. I had one doctor who thought I was only there to get medicine to get high, so he told me in front of my son that he was prescribing Narcan, *"just in case I overdosed,"* since *"nothing appeared to be medically wrong"* with me. That day, I hobbled out of the doctor's office, holding onto my son's arms with tears in my eyes. The pain was getting worse, yet no one seemed to believe me. One day, I received a message from the doctor stating, *"I will order an X-ray of your back, even though I do not think we will find anything."*

I went in for the appointment to have the X-rays taken. Shortly after, a nurse called me with the results. I had Neuropathy, Degenerative Disc, Spinal Stenosis, Incapacitated Chronic Pain, and Arthritis in my spine. There is no cure for any of those conditions. I had a choice to continue taking medicine, get acupuncture, take physical therapy, or receive trigger shots and then get surgery. I am so thankful for my praying sons, sorority sisters, and church family. I opted to receive the trigger shots, but they didn't work. Surgery was on the table, but I decided not to proceed. My doctor updated my medical chart and put in the notes: **"Permanently Disabled."** I still struggle with that diagnosis... that *label*. Even as I am writing this, tears have formed in my eyes. But my God is able. My God is **faithful**.

Today, I am trying to get used to my new normal. I have good days and bad ones, but I am still here! I know that God has a plan for my life and that all those things will work out for my good because I am a called and chosen woman of God. He holds and strengthens me when I believe, even when I waver in my belief.

So, my reader, whatever you are going through, make sure you are going through it with Jesus. He will never leave you or forsake you. And who knows? Maybe your name came up, and God trusts you enough to let you go through "IT" to show the enemy that you will not give up, no matter what comes your way, because your hope rests in God.

*"Now, there was a day when the sons of God came to present themselves before the Lord, and Satan also came among them. The Lord said to Satan, 'From where have you come?' Satan answered the Lord and said, 'From going to and fro on the earth, and from walking up and down on it.' And the Lord said to Satan, **'Have you considered my servant Job,** that there is none like him on the earth, a blameless and upright man, who fears God and turns away from evil?'"* (Job 6:6-8, ESV)

In the Depths of Pain – A Poem

Genae Kulah © 2024

In the depths of pain, when shadows loom,
And the heart feels heavy, lost in gloom,
I lift my eyes to the heavens high,
For in my sorrow, Lord, You are nigh.

When tears flow freely, like a river wide,
I seek Your comfort, my faithful guide.
In every ache, in every sigh,
I feel Your presence, Lord, standing by.

Though storms may rage, and winds may howl,
In the quiet whisper, I hear Your vow:
"Fear not, dear child, for I am here.
In times of trouble, I draw you near."

When doubts assail, and faith feels weak,
Your Word becomes the strength I seek.
For You, O Lord, are my refuge strong;
In the darkest night, You sing my song.

You turn my mourning into dance.
With every struggle, You give me a chance,
To trust in Your plans, though I cannot see,
For Your ways are higher, Your love sets me free.

So, in the pain, I'll choose to stand,
With an open heart and outstretched hand.
For You are faithful, my hope, my guide;
In the midst of the pain, I will abide.

With every trial, You shape my soul.
In Your loving arms, I am made whole.
I'll trust in You through joy and strife,
For You are the healer, the giver of life.

PRECIOUS DAMAS

Dedication: I dedicate this to God for being so faithful to me and never turning his back on me, even when I sin. He is the only one who can keep a promise and never disappoint me. I will always be His daughter and keep my faith. I love You, Lord.

Bio: Precious Damas is a Wife, Mother, Grandmother, Daughter, Auntie, and Sister Best Friend. Born and raised in Massachusetts, she is a dedicated Boston Celtics fan. She is the Author of the Mask Off book series and has co-authored true-life stories in the God's Fruit series, which made the International Bestseller list. Her mantra is, *"I am Precious. I was born Precious, and I will die Precious! It gets no more real than that!"* Follow her literary journey by connecting with her at https://www.facebook.com/MaskOffSeries.

I Am Job

I have always believed in God but rarely attended church as a child. As a teenager, I only went to get out of the house. Admittedly, I didn't really know what I was looking for; I just knew there was a God and heard He sent His only Begotten Son, Jesus, to die for our sins. In a nutshell, that's all I knew. I can honestly say I was taught the first chapter of the Bible (Genesis), and it seemed to stop around there. I knew the story of Adam and Eve and that their sons' names were Cain and Abel. When I learned about Moses, **THAT'S** when things got a bit more interesting! After seeing God's work on parting the Red Sea, I knew God was real—and that's all I needed to know. From then on, I tried to be a perfect child by being humble, upright, honest, and fair. As I got older, I heard about Jesus from the elders in my family. I also went to church a few times with my friends, but whenever I saw the grownups jumping up and down and speaking another language, I was scared. *(Can you say cult-like?)* I kid you not!

I encourage you to read my story in *God's Kindness Fruit* (the book before this one in the *God's Fruit* series). If you do, you will learn I went through some things early in my Christian walk. You will learn that I prayed a lot and tried to activate my faith, all while not fully understanding or truly knowing who God was. For me, praying was simply talking to myself and hoping to get home safely.

In early adulthood, my first son was born into an era when gangs of young men "owned territories and gunned each other down if you wore the wrong color in their neighborhood." The neighborhood was under siege and unsafe. Once again, I talked to myself and prayed to a divine being I didn't even know, trying to activate my faith.

I guess my choice to live an upright life paid off, though. I witnessed my daughter and sons graduate from high school when some of their peers didn't live to see the day. May they rest in peace.

At one point, the party scene with my girlfriends was the life I chose to live. We spent our time drinking, gossiping, and having outright fun! Yes, I was sinning, but at the same time, I remained humble, honest, and fair. I was not out there stealing, killing, or ruining my body like many of my peers. I just wanted to have fun—but something was missing in my life. I wanted more and was kind of upset that what I wanted wasn't coming fast enough.

****

My Daily Bread

I am writing this story on June 9, 2024. Earlier today, I attended church services and received my daily bread from the pastor.

The pastor preached about God's faithful servant, Job, and how he lost everything within an estimated 30-minute span. Job lost his cattle, donkeys, and servants. He received that information from one of his servants who survived the attack. As Job received that devastating news, another servant approached and gave Job more upsetting news: his sheep and remaining servants died in a fire. Just when he thought it couldn't get any worse, yet another servant reported the worst of all: a mighty wind came and collapsed the house of his oldest son, killing all his children. The devastation was vast and hit Job hard. In response, he ripped off his clothes and fell to his knees, saying:

"*Naked I came from my mother's womb, and naked I will depart. The LORD gave, and the LORD has taken away; may the name of the LORD be praised*" (Job 1:21, NIV).

Job never lost his faith in God because he knew and trusted Him. All that was taken from Job was not because of sin, though. Remember: Job was an honest, humble, and upright man! Nonetheless, he realized he was not without sin, so he repented and was rewarded by having everything replaced anew—his wife, family, and wealth. Job had built his foundation from the bedrock, which held him steadfast in his belief and faith.

Setting My Foundation

In my case, the losses were a bit different and hit differently. It went something like this: I started building my faith in God on bedrock *after* losing six people near and dear to me, two of them being my gym brothers.

Then…

In March 2022, I lost my mother to lung cancer. People say that we can never truly be prepared, but I was. I miss you, Ma. R.I.P.

Then…

In June 2022, I lost my nephew to Fentanyl. That was when I started digging to build my foundation. (If you read my story in *God's Kindness Fruit*, you will see how I fell to my knees, collapsed in my husband's arms, and came out of my clothes, just like Job.) For one minute and 36 seconds, my spirit departed my body.

Then…

In July 2022, I lost my uncle while still in shock about my nephew. In fact, funeral arrangements were still being made for my nephew when my uncle passed away.

Then…

In August 2022, after returning home from vacation, I received a call at work from my cousin informing me that her brother died.

Sidebar: As I reflected on setting my foundation on bedrock, one of the first things that came to mind was the cartoon "The Flintstones." Funny, I know.

Seriously, though. It's important to note that from an engineering perspective, to build a foundation, you must dig all the way down to the bedrock to secure the hold. That's what I did. I dug deep and started building my faith in God.

As I attended my cousin's homegoing service, I had no more tears to shed. I was all cried out. I recall sitting there speechless and sucking up my grief while supporting my cousins. It was hard to do. I was muted as I sat in the corner and thought, *"I can't handle any more grief!"* I can't say I was mad at God, but I did question Him and tried to understand why all that happened. I remained mute for weeks afterward, waiting for an answer. Was God trying to get my attention? I had hoped to hear from Him soon! In the Bible, we are instructed to be still and wait patiently for the LORD. Well, I waited… and waited… and waited until one Sunday, I decided to go to church. I thought, *"I'll hear from God there."* After months of attending and not hearing from God, something in my spirit told me to get out of there, so I did.

Some weeks passed, and while corresponding with a good friend, she told me, *"God will lead you. Just wait."* I waited a few more weeks before being led to the church of the pastor who officiated the services of my deceased family members. Instantly, I felt at home and knew I wasn't going anywhere else. God was right there, leading and speaking to me. His faithfulness started to bloom in me! My healing journey had begun!

I continued to go to church and attend weekly Bible studies. My mission was to get as close to God as possible, so I put my life in God's hands. In the process, I became a new person. I "walked out of my grave clothes and into a new robe"! I walked differently, felt different, and spoke differently. God was right there with me the entire time. As I overcame my grief and disbelief, I knew God had a plan for me after putting me through some trying times. I decided I would no longer sit in my pity because I knew the loved ones I had lost were resting in a better place.

I must insert a slight pause in my story here. I questioned myself about that saying, "They're in a better place." Are they? If a person lived a good life but was not baptized, can we say they're truly in a better place when they depart from us? What if they were murdered or died from a drug overdose but were not baptized? Are they in a better place? How does God make His decision concerning those instances? We will never know the answer on this side of Heaven.

Back to my story.

After my mom departed from this life, she visited me with so many beautiful signs and dreams. My nephew also came. I felt his presence sitting on the edge of my bed. Both played a significant part in my healing. God's faithfulness was in full effect. He knew I sought understanding. He knew no one could answer my questions. I felt so alone, but I started to feel God's unchanging hands on me. My faith grew stronger, and I knew He kept his promises concerning me when I prayed to Him. It was He who brought me through it all—God's faithfulness at its finest!

Eventually, I became much calmer and felt at peace. Nothing bothered me because I knew God had me. I really got to know Him for myself. The evidence of His faithfulness is real! He wakes me up, keeps me calm, and gives me peace, no matter what I face on any given day. Listen up: God doesn't play about me! He reminds me daily who He is and what He has done for me. When I'm wrong, I repent and am honest with Him. I love it when God showers me with His faithfulness!

I remember a moment when I was young, and God pulled me out of temptation when I was in the wrong place at the wrong time. He showed up in my time of suffering and saved me. I recall crying myself to sleep when I was in a dark place, and no one even knew—but GOD knew I needed to rest so that He could work on me. Although I didn't know Him like I do now, I knew He was the G.O.A.T. (Greatest Of All Time) and would make things better. I refused to be one of those people who used God to get out of a bind and then throw Him aside until they were in yet another bind. I knew better than that.

Many are familiar with the story of Jesus walking on water toward the boat Peter and the other disciples were on in Matthew 14. When they saw Him coming, they couldn't believe their eyes! Peter called out to Jesus and said, *"If it is You, tell me to come to You."* Jesus replied, *"Come to me."* Peter headed out to

Jesus, walking on the water until the wind started blowing. Right then and there, Peter lost a little bit of his faith.

Dear reader, losing faith in God only takes a slight distraction. I encourage you to keep steadfast faith in God, no matter what! Let nothing distract you or keep you from being devoted and loyal to God or your belief in Him. God is an unfailing God, a faithful God, and worthy of your praise, honor, and glory. Get to know who God is. Know that He is always on time and never late. He is your great defender. He is the day, and He is the night. He is the Alpha and Omega, the Beginning and the End. He is a waymaker for all who believe in Him. He will remove roadblocks that no one else can. How do I know? I am a living testimony of it all!

"The LORD is trustworthy in all he promises and faithful in all He does" (Psalm 145:13, NIV).

My mother had a saying that remains with me to this day. Even though she had her trials and tribulations, she always dropped gems on my siblings and me. Her favorite (and perhaps most memorable) was, *"You better thank God! Thank Him every day, Precious!"* I now see why she wanted me to do just that. She helped prepare me for my own trials and tribulations and the knowledge that God's faithfulness would get me through them.

Allow God's faithfulness to bloom all over you, my friend!

TOSHA R. DEARBONE

Dedication: I dedicate my story to all who have felt as though God has left their side. To my children: God is with you. He will never leave you. Let my story be a testimony that life may happen, but we have a Heavenly Father who remains faithful in our lives.

Bio: Tosha Dearbone was born in Louisiana and raised in Missouri City, Texas. She is a mother of four and grandmother of two. For the last 18 years, she has worked in the medical field with adolescents at Texas Children's Hospital. She also mentors youths within the juvenile system and was recently promoted to the Youth Director at Transforming Faith Christian Center. Tosha utilizes her experience in the medical field by educating young ladies and women about HIV and AIDS, domestic and sexual violence, and building self-esteem. To connect with Tosha, follow her on social media at Tosha R Dearbone and via email at trdearbo@yahoo.com.

God's Faithfulness Caused Me to Grow Up

From the very beginning, as a little girl, I have paid attention to how God has been amazingly faithful in my life. I invite you to come and walk with me through the fields of grace and mercy in bloom.

Reflecting on my childhood, I first recognized God's faithfulness at the age of seven, even while I was afraid to speak up about the abuse I endured. My abuser (a cousin) directed me to touch him inappropriately as early as age seven. That was the first time I noticed God didn't allow that situation to ruin me. Instead, God kept me close to Him and continued to walk the journey with me.

You see, my father passed away shortly after the molestation took place from complications with his own health. What a heartbreaking situation that was for me. I remember the day well. My little brother and I were picked up from school, only to arrive at the hospital to face a door with a heart on it. Shortly after, we were told, *"Your daddy has already passed away."* Immediately, tears began to flow from the wells of my eyes. All I could think was, **"Who will protect me now?"**

Allow me to back up for just a moment and share about the time when I first spoke up about the abuse. Many people often asked why I didn't speak up and tell someone. Well, I was more afraid of what my father would have done to my cousin or, perhaps worse, my father getting hurt behind what someone else did to me. Keeping quiet was my safe space. Still, thoughts plagued my young mind, such as, *"There's no need to get my father involved and possibly sent to jail or have something else happen to him because of someone else's foolishness."* Disappointingly, the sexual abuse didn't stop there. It continued with multiple other people, yet God remained faithful. He was still right there with me, doing just as He said he would. He protected me.

Years went by, and I became pregnant at age 15. With no hesitation, I was told, *"You are getting an abortion."* I had no adversary, so I gave in to the demand without any understanding of how it would impact my life. Imagine for just a moment: The thought of ending a pregnancy can be traumatic, especially as you begin to feel as though something heavy is weighing on you. As for me, I began to ponder on the fundamental question in my mind: **Did I really end a life?** The guilt, the shame, the pressure, and the happiness to sadness that occurred sent me through a whirlwind. Thought after thought arose, and question after question plagued me. I wondered, **"Is God mad at me? What did I just do?"** I cried hysterically, overwhelmed by the entire thing, until I heard a still, small voice whisper, *"You are not the sin. This sin doesn't belong to you."*

"'For I know the plans I have for you,' declared the Lord, 'plans to prosper you and not to harm you, plans to give you hope and a future'" (Jeremiah 29:11, NIV).

After hearing God's voice, I cried happy tears — tears of joy, knowing that God was not mad at me. Instead, it was a part of His plan all along. Whew! Talk about a release of emotions and feelings of defeat as I remembered that God is always on my side!

In 1996, I was faced with another pregnancy at the tender age of sixteen. My God! I was so afraid to tell my momma because, just the year before, I experienced a level of pain I never wanted to endure again. I'll never forget the way she looked at me when I opened my mouth to give her the news. She wasted no time asking me, *"So, what are you going to do?"*

With tears in my eyes, I opened my mouth and uttered the words, *"I'm going to keep it."* Her silence was enough to make me start praying internally. ***"Dear God, I need You. Please don't have her make me go through that horrible experience again."*** Well, God showed up in her silence. With no idea what to expect, my real journey forged ahead.

On February 11, 1997, a baby girl entered this world, and my need to feel wanted was fulfilled. I now had someone who would love me and accept me unconditionally in her life. However, things were still a bit shaky at home, and all I could think of was how to get out. I didn't want anyone to feel obligated to be responsible for my child. I needed to be independent and show others what I could do.

Roughly two months later, I figured out a plan and put it into play, all while asking God to continue to guide me through the fields of grace and mercy. The first thing I did was seek housing for my daughter and me. I applied for Section 8 housing assistance but was told I made $1,000.00 too much. Talk about being puzzled and confused! **BUT GOD!** He was still faithful to me. He saw fit for us to move into a two-bedroom apartment as he continued to order my steps. I worked, cared for my baby girl, and still attended high school — all of them feats no one thought I could do. Two years after my daughter's birth, I got pregnant again. I just knew things would get hard, but God showed up again and reminded me that He was always with me.

Fast forward a bit...

I was doing well and living well, all while struggling mentally about my experiences as a young girl up until young adulthood. Yes, your girl went through some stuff. I hoped God would clean me up and make it as though nothing ever happened. Regardless of the rejection, thoughts of abandonment, abuse, and becoming a teen mother with no support from my children's fathers, I was able to keep going.

So, it's not an understatement when I say that God's faithfulness caused me to grow up. I would have never thought that becoming a teen mom would be the catalyst that thrust me into maturity and made me want to know more about who God is.

There were times when I suffered from suicidal thoughts and attempts. I remember wanting to take my life at 16, 19, 24, and 28 years old. The time when I was 24, I think about often because that was when I recognized God's hands covering me. Come with me back to that time…

One morning, as I was preparing for work, I and the dude I was talking to at the time got into a heated argument, and thoughts of rejection and abandonment started messing with my mind. I ran to the restroom, looking for a bottle of Tylenol (my go-to pill to try and cease the pain). Within seconds, I had taken almost a whole bottle. Shortly after, I proceeded to work at around 6:00 a.m. I remember pulling into the parking garage, but I don't recall calling anyone. I then passed out. By the grace of God, when I woke up, it was maybe 10:00 or 11:00 p.m., and I was home in my bed. I looked around, trying to figure out how I got there. I was so confused. Why didn't anyone take me to the hospital? Was anyone even checking on me? I never got the answer to those questions, but I did learn that I had called my guy friend before passing out, which was how he knew where to come and get me. Praise God!

As I think back on that day, I am always reminded of just how faithful God has been to me. He has never left me, and He has never allowed me to remain in a defeated position. He makes a way, even when I can't see it. God is a faithful Father. He is also a God of follow-through. He navigates you and me through the fields of grace and mercy daily.

I imagine you're probably wondering if I ever sought help. Well, I did.

In 2018, the enemy tried to come against me again—that time, it was in the form of hopelessness. I attempted to overdose on pills once again, but I somehow found the courage to laugh out loud as if someone had told me a joke, not realizing I was actually entertaining angels unaware. Those angels protected me and brought with them a sense of peace.

Throughout that evening, I pondered how to seek mental health support and remembered that my job had a program to help employees. The next day, I approached my manager and asked for the information, with no idea she would share her own story with me. *I hope by now you can see how God steps in.* After listening to her victorious story, I proceeded to the Employees' Assistance Program office. I will never forget the day. When I entered the office, the woman asked, *"What is going on?"* I began to tell her about my suicidal thoughts and feeling like I wasn't enough. She then asked, *"What do you do outside of work?"*

"I operate a nonprofit for girls and go inside the juvenile centers to mentor girls and boys," I replied.

She got on her computer and Googled me before turning around and asking, *"Is this the same person?"*

"Yes," I said.

"This can't be because this person has so much purpose!" she exclaimed. I immediately began to cry. She then spoke to me about therapy and medication.

Without hesitation, I blurted out, *"No medicine, just therapy, please."*

She picked up the phone and called a therapist. Right then and there, an appointment was scheduled for me. *"This never happens this way,"* she said thoughtfully. *"The therapist typically doesn't answer the phone and usually doesn't have immediate appointments available."* Wow! All I could do was cry and thank God because He did it again! He continued to show up for me!

I attended the scheduled appointment and continued to see the therapist for about a month because she said I was already doing the work to heal. *"When you started the nonprofit, your healing and deliverance journey began,"* she stated. **My God.** I'm grateful for her because she helped me identify my triggers and learn how to set boundaries, both areas where I was lacking.

Through the sharing of my testimony, I want to remind someone who may be struggling with thoughts of hopelessness and suicide that you are loved. You are wanted. You are accepted, and God is a faithful Father. He will not leave you or forsake you, for His Word stands with truth, grace, and mercy to help you navigate life, for His Word says:

"Thy word is a lamp unto my feet, and a light unto my path" (Psalm 119:105, KJV).

God's faithfulness caused me to grow up. He did it for me, and He can do it for you. Begin to look at every situation not as what you can receive but as what you can bring. With

God's faithfulness, He has already equipped you with more than enough. That, my friend, is the faithfulness of the Holy One.

LAURIE BENOIT

Dedication: To those who have shown me the true meaning of faithfulness, loyalty, and trust: Your unwavering support and genuine care have been my pillars of strength. This chapter is dedicated to you with heartfelt gratitude for the lessons and love you have shared.

Bio: Laurie Benoit is a survivor who has experienced both beauty and chaos. After years of abuse, she has emerged with resilience, courage, and compassion. Her mission is to raise awareness about the effects of abuse, support others in their healing process, advocate for change, and remind everyone that they are not alone on their journey. Laurie's work combines the transformative power of words with nature's peaceful energy. Her Internationally Bestselling book, *The Transformative Power of "The Word,"* is a hauntingly moving testament to her path of healing and inspiration. You can connect with her on Facebook at Once Awakened.

The Pillars of Faithfulness: Loyalty, Trust, and Respect

Faithfulness (noun): **The quality of being faithful; fidelity.**

When you think of faithfulness, what comes to mind? Marriage vows? The loyalty of a beloved pet? Or perhaps the unwavering trust in a close friend?

For me, in its simplest terms, faithfulness equates to loyalty. It is something that has always been deeply instilled in my soul since my very first memories. So, imagine how deeply disheartening it was when I discovered that not everyone developed that same level of loyalty or faithfulness. In fact, my very first lesson concerning faithfulness was within the family structure (or, perhaps I should say, the lack thereof).

In my family, faithfulness meant nothing. The façade of pedigree and perfection took precedence over genuine loyalty and care. And so, as I reflect on those days, it should come as no surprise that I would hold no faithfulness for a family that cared to have none for me in return. I learned that well from my one sibling, who protected their own "best interests" over their one and only younger sibling and continues to do so to this day.

Here's my painful truth: Because there was no faithfulness within my family structure, my first and deepest pains in life came from them, leaving me with an even deeper lack of loyalty and care for the word "family."

As a child, however, when I encountered my first day of school, I pledged faithfulness to a young girl who changed my very horrifying first day into one of the most memorable days of my life. That same young girl saved me from many more painstaking days in the years to come. You see, my first day consisted of being late and enduring a very embarrassing moment that would become a reason to be bullied. The kids used to taunt me with hurtful names that made me feel deep sadness and pain. It was as if they were discriminating against me, making me feel like there was something wrong with who I was. Their hurtful words, coupled with the childhood trauma I was enduring, fueled my pain even more.

As the years passed, "family" became a distant and vacant word in my life, and friendships would later become my chosen family. Faithfulness was something I pledged to only a genuine few along the way.

"Faithfulness is not just a virtue; it's a testament to the strength of one's character and the depth of one's soul." ~ Laurie Benoit © 2024

That quote is a truth that has proven evident in my life. As such, faithfulness has been reserved for genuinely authentic individuals who have proven beyond a measure of doubt that they deserve it.

I have learned that faithfulness can manifest in many different aspects and situations in life. As a homeless youth living on the streets, I found that there was a certain amount of faithfulness or loyalty even within the "street cliques." That was crucial for my survival, especially when I found myself being hunted by a prostitution and human trafficking ring. During that perilous time, I met someone who answered my call for help and provided me with a means to escape. That marked the end of my journey as a homeless street youth, but it also forged a bond of faithfulness in a friendship that has endured for nearly 40 years.

After escaping from the streets, I was eager to attempt to live a normal life when I was introduced to "Hal." Our courtship began and seemed to be going smoothly until, after some time, he started inquiring about my "friends." Of course, as adults, we want to meet our partner's friends, but he started asking barely a month later. When I made the same request, he coldly shut me down with a snappy retort: *"You already know my one friend – my boss."* Even though I left it alone, he didn't. He insisted on meeting at least one of my friends, so I introduced him to "Kay." Why did I choose her? Because I believed she and I had a deep bonding friendship and hoped that he, too, was faithful to me. But time would eventually reveal that neither held the same depth of faithfulness that I had for them, and it crushed me.

Some might think faithfulness should be given freely and not be an earned attribute, but in my life, giving too much to some has caused deep-seated pain. Yes, I believe that in some instances, faithfulness should be expressed and shown without a doubt, like in the case of marriage. Still, that is a two-way street, too. There must be a mutual respect that two people have for one another, just as it should be in family and friendship. You can't expect faithfulness when you don't extend that respect to others. That's not to say it's okay to hurt another because of a lack of faithfulness. As I mentioned, it comes down to simple respect. If one person does not share the same belief, problems can arise. Mutuality is key.

Once again, I return to the many different lessons of faithfulness I have experienced. This next part of my journey reveals yet another path and lesson in faithfulness.

Years passed, and when I finally felt stable enough to commit to full-time employment, I began my job search, which led me to the retail industry—a field I had never explored but found intriguing. I was still in my young womanhood, so I had plenty of inexperience but was eager to broaden my knowledge. I was fortunate enough to find a job and be hired as a management trainee right off the bat. Wow! What luck! In truth, it was exactly where I was meant to be at that moment in time.

I worked for a woman who was deeply passionate about her job and her company. Her mentorship was invaluable, and I quickly learned to share her enthusiasm and zest for the work. I became a faithful employee, working diligently and learning from her. In return, she showed immense faithfulness to me. I remained with her for over a year until I became pregnant with my second child. Unfortunately, morning sickness made it difficult to continue working, so I resigned.

For the faithfulness I displayed in the workplace, my boss always asked my potential employers to pass along words of kindness to me whenever they called for a reference. Her kindness and support have never left my heart or thoughts, even though she has long since passed away. That experience remains one of the finest examples of mutual faithfulness in my life, but that was far from the end of my lessons about faithfulness.

In the year that followed, faithfulness would rise to meet me once again, not long after I had my second child. I'm fairly certain I wasn't the only woman to ever experience postpartum depression. With years of built-up childhood trauma that had yet to be healed, I was very self-conscious and insecure about my body and self-image. Although I longed to be a better parent than either of mine, I felt my life spiraling out of control. It didn't help that my spouse wanted an "open relationship" and kept trying to pressure me into wanting the same, but I didn't. The more pressure I received, the more my insecurities surfaced. My childhood traumas began to resurface, bringing feelings of neglect and not being good enough, followed by floods of rage.

Then came the final straw.

One evening, as my spouse and I sat watching TV, there was a knock on the door. He went to answer it, and when I inquired about the visitor, I was told they had left—but they hadn't. My spouse then said he was going to take a shower, and I thought nothing of it. When the shower stopped, around the corner came not one but two people: him and a woman I absolutely wanted nothing to do with, both fresh out of the shower.

Faithfulness

As you might imagine, faithfulness was not a word I had at that very moment. Shocked and appalled would have been mild words to describe my feelings. When asked if I wished to join them, loathing rage boiled below the surface. *"I'm leaving,"* was all I could blurt out.

I hastily packed up my children, called a recently reconnected friend from years ago who I knew when I was in foster care, and asked if I could flee to her place. Of course, she opened her doors to me. *What I hadn't known then was what it would cost me.* Another lesson in faithfulness was on the horizon, and it would be in the making for well over a year.

Friendship

In my experience, we sometimes get the impression that people are on the same level of friendship when, in reality, we're nowhere near on the same level. That was a profound lesson in friendship and faithfulness I was about to learn.

The friend who took me in with my two children appeared supportive until I was faced with the decision of having to leave my children with their father simply because I had no outside support. She tried to convince me it was best to take the kids for "survival" purposes (in other words, to collect welfare, child support, and child tax credits). But to me, my kids were not a paycheck; they were little people who needed the love and support I felt I couldn't give them as a single parent with no support system in place. So, I left my children with their father, knowing they would have the family support I couldn't provide. Truth be told, it was the hardest decision of my life. Have I regretted it? Absolutely. Every day of my life. Although they are "in my life," they really are not a part of my life and have never been able to move past that pain toward me. Perhaps one day...

Back to my *"faithfulness in friendship"* lesson.

Not long after I gave up the kids, I chose to move to another city with my "friend" and her children. In doing so, I was truly about to see the depth of what our friendship meant to her. The thing was, it wasn't just her and I moving to another city; it was her and I, her new boyfriend, his friend who owned a vehicle, and her three young boys. As soon as we began our journey, our relationship quickly became about money. Unbeknownst to me, I was expected to pay for half of the food, gas, ferry costs, lodging, and whatever else was needed along the way. But it didn't end there. After my money was used up and she and the others still had money left, threats came that I would be left with my belongings on the side of the road unless I provided extra money. I was taken to a pawn shop and told to pawn what little I had. That included a few rings, a custom-made original ring that was a gift from my mother, and a couple of gold necklaces. After I had done that, I was told I didn't have enough money for food, so I did without.

I should have been well aware that things were headed downhill very quickly. Instead of getting out of there with what little I had left, I believed my friend would ease up once we got settled. Wow, was I ever wrong!

After arriving in the new city, I applied for a job the very next day and was hired on the spot. In fact, I started working immediately after I was hired. Talk about luck!

From a hotel room that we rented, I continued to work. My "friend" applied for welfare, and because she had kids, they accepted her into the system. Since I was already working, she offered me to move in with them, saying we would "work out the details after settling in." As it turned out, she and her partner rented a three-bedroom apartment because it was within their budget, which was great! Since my friend had three young boys, herself, and her partner, I fully expected them to take at least two bedrooms, leaving one of us other adults to have the third room. That was not how it worked out.

This is when things really played out.

Three weeks passed, and I received my first paycheck. My boss drove me to a bank to cash my check and then took me back to the apartment. That day, I saw exactly what my friendship meant to my "friend." Because I had gotten home late, I was grilled about why I was late. Then came the questions about my paycheck and the truth of her expectations. In my absence, all three adults apparently discussed what was fair for me to pay. I was informed that because I was working, it was "my duty" to pay half the rent, half the bills, and half the food. **Uh. Wow! Wait! What?** Right then, she demanded I pay my rent in full and that whatever money I had left could be put towards bills, food, etc. In short, I was told, *"Hand over your paycheck."* I had some serious issues with that and asked, **"How do you expect I get to work?"**

Then came the snotty retort: *"Well, if your boss can drive you home, she can pick you up, too."* I didn't say anything more. I just handed her most of my paycheck and told her she was not getting the rest because I still had to get to work, like it or not. The next day, when I returned home from work, my "friend" passed me an envelope with a letter directing me to vacate their apartment within 24 hours.

I didn't wait for the allotted time. I left that night. I recall walking for hours until I came across a bar. Call it luck, the universe, or whatever you like, but as I sat there contemplating what to do, I just so happened to run into someone I knew from my hometown. She immediately recognized me and invited me to her table to catch up. I shared everything that had happened since I last saw her, including my separation from my ex and up to that night. She gave me her number and said, *"Call me from work tomorrow. I'll see what I can do."* The next day, without any rent money to my name, she helped me move into a place I would call home for at least two years.

When I tried to retrieve my belongings from my "friend," she never answered the door and never tried to contact me until about two months later after I called her. When we spoke, she apologized and offered me my belongings. What she didn't tell me was the condition they were in. She had taken a knife and literally destroyed my belongings. She sliced them to shreds!

That harsh lesson of faithfulness in friendship became an etched memory for my lifetime.

****

Reflecting on those experiences, I have come to understand that faithfulness is not just about loyalty to others but also about being true to oneself. The harsh lessons I learned from those who betrayed my trust have only strengthened my resolve to surround myself with genuine, caring individuals. While the journey has been fraught with challenges, it has also been a testament to my resilience and capacity for growth.

I have realized that faithfulness is a precious gift that must be earned and cherished. Through the trials, I have found my true pillars of **Loyalty, Trust, and Respect.**

JOURNAL YOUR FAITH WALK

For the next 30 days, you are encouraged to journal those things you are "faithing" for in the following section. Leave room to annotate when that item was realized, and give God the glory for showing you favor by fulfilling your request.

God's Faithfulness Fruit: Walking Through the Fields of Grace and Mercy in Bloom

God's Faithfulness Fruit: Walking Through the Fields of Grace and Mercy in Bloom

God's Faithfulness Fruit: Walking Through the Fields of Grace and Mercy in Bloom

God's Faithfulness Fruit: Walking Through the Fields of Grace and Mercy in Bloom

God's Faithfulness Fruit: Walking Through the Fields of Grace and Mercy in Bloom

ABOUT THE COMPILER

Angela R. Edwards is the CEO and Chief Editorial Director of Pearly Gates Publishing, LLC (PGP) and Redemption's Story Publishing, LLC (RSP) — Award-winning International Hybrid Christian Publishing Houses located in the Central Savannah River Area of Georgia. In May 2018, PGP was honored as the 2018 Winner of Distinction for Publishing in South Houston, Texas, by the Better Business Bureau (BBB). From 2018 to the present day, she has been the recipient of BBB's Gold Star Certificate for both entities for her exemplary service to the community.

Angela lives by *"My Words Have POWER!"* Since its inception in January 2015, PGP has been blessed with an ever-growing and diverse group of over 100 authors who have penned topics related to faith, love, abuse, bullying, Christian fiction, Bible study tools, marriage, and so much more. Their youngest author is two years old; their eldest is 83 at the time of this publication. To their credit and God's glory, PGP and RSP have collectively over 150 bestselling titles to date, including a series penned by Mr. Jimmy Merchant, formerly of the 1950s Doo-Wop group, "Frankie Lymon & The Teenagers," with their most recognizable music hit, *Why Do Fools Fall in Love*.

An affordable publishing option (in comparison to some of the large, traditional publishing houses), PGP and RSP work one-on-one with authors, ensuring that financial hardship is not a discouraging part of the publishing process. For those desiring to share their God-inspired messages, to include both new and seasoned authors, both publishing houses provide unique services and support that many have said "left them feeling as if they were the only author" placed under each company's care.

The Holy Bible states that *"God loves a cheerful giver"* (2 Corinthians 9:7). To that end, PGP and RSP are frequently hosting fantastic giveaways. Throughout the past few years, new author contests have awarded authors over $18,000.00 in services collectively.

In addition to the aforementioned, Angela is a domestic abuse survivor. Since first telling her abuse survivor story publicly, she has become a "Trumpet for Change." She is the Founder of the Battle-Scar Free Movement—a 501(c)(3) nonprofit that provides resources to abuse victims and survivors as they transition to a life free from abuse. As part of her God-given mission, she provided abuse victims and survivors a FREE opportunity to anonymously share their testimonies in a seven-book series titled *God Says I am Battle-Scar Free*. Although the series is complete, Angela's mission to help individuals heal with the power of their words continues. Assisting others with the healing process is paramount to her, which propelled her into volunteering for two years at the Star of Hope Mission in Houston, Texas, as their first-ever Domestic Violence Liaison.

Angela holds an A.A. degree in Business Administration from the University of Phoenix and is pursuing her B.S. degree in Psychology with a concentration in Christian Counseling from LeTourneau University. She is a woman of God, wife, mother, grandmother of 23, and trusted friend. Originally a New Jersey native, she has since made Georgia her home and embraced the southern culture in all its fullness.

Angela loves life and affirms daily: *"NOT TODAY, SATAN! AND TOMORROW ISN'T LOOKING TOO GOOD, EITHER!"*

CONTACT THE PUBLISHER

Pearly Gates Publishing and Redemption's Story Publishing are always looking for new talent and desire to "birth the writer" in **YOU**! Will you be next on their list of **Bestselling Authors?**

Contact us today!

Visit PGP on the Web at PearlyGatesPublishing.com
Visit RSP on the Web at Redemptions-Story.com
Connect with PGP on Facebook at
Pearly Gates Publishing
Connect with RSP on Facebook at
Redemptions Story Publishing
Email Angela Edwards, CEO at
pearlygatespublishing@gmail.com

Call 832-994-8797 to schedule a FREE 15-minute publishing consultation.

****

The Battle-Scar Free Movement
can be found on the Web at
Bsfmovement.org
and on Facebook at
Bsfmovement

www.ingramcontent.com/pod-product-compliance
Lightning Source LLC
Chambersburg PA
CBHW071212160426
43196CB00011B/2271